The Pit of Success

Praise for *The Pit of Success*

"Powerful and practical…*The Pit of Success* is a must read for today's leaders. I highly recommend it! You will never have to worry about plateauing as a leader or an organization if you apply these principles. Jennings and Leishman give the mindset, skillset, and toolset every leader needs to accelerate their learning curve and grow their business."

—**Sean Covey**, President, FranklinCovey Education
and *New York Times* Best-Selling author

"Insightful and relevant…Backed by theory, grounded in research, and drawing on experience, this is a must use set of ideas. *The Pit of Success* gives leaders—and all people—the ability to reinvent, reimagine, and transform their future success. The engaging stories and useful tools provide a path for day-to-day actions."

—**Dave Ulrich**, *New York Times* Best-Selling author
and #1 Most Influential Global HR Leader

"Relatable and applicable for everyone…no matter what stage you are in life or in your career. *The Pit of Success* takes the concept of the innovator's dilemma to a personal level and helps leaders to let go of what got them here and learn to lead for the new marketplace. This is going to be so helpful for so many people."

—**Andrea Leszek**, Senior Vice President
and Chief Operations Officer, Salesforce

"Real personal growth requires leaving behind the very things that got you the success you've enjoyed so far, demanding that you take on unfamiliar tasks and roles that can feel scary and unrewarding. Jennings and Leishman's delightful new book helps you realize that everybody faces the same challenges and feelings – not just you – and offers straightforward practices to help you navigate."

—**Rita McGrath**, Best-Selling author of *Seeing Around Corners: How to Spot Inflection Points in Business Before they Happen*

"Highly recommend! *The Pit of Success* highlights, and helps anyone overcome, a critical dilemma: that your core skills and expertise can become a roadblock to overcoming your next challenge. The principles shared here will help you become a life-long learner who can overcome each new challenge."

—**Jeff Dyer**, Best-Selling author, *The Innovator's DNA*

"Learning to learn is truly the master skill we all need. Jennings and Leishman offer powerful and practical tools to help us move through the pit of success with mastery and develop the mental strength we need to tackle the next set of challenges."

—**Liz Wiseman**, Best-Selling author of *Multipliers* and *Rookie Smarts*

"An inspiring framework that delivers tangible results... *The Pit of Success* is an invaluable resource full of practical advice and tools that will help you find the courage to take on new challenges with vigor and overcome the fears of taking on demanding roles. I look forward to sharing with our leaders who have already significantly benefited from the trainings."

—**Jayne Hart**, Executive Vice President, Myriad Genetics

"Compelling and enlightening...the kind of book that stays with you over time. I have found as much benefit in both my personal and work life as any book I have read. I wish I would have understood this at the start of my career but fortunately I can apply it to my next pit of success."

—**Bernie Tobin**, General Manager, Natera-Precision Medicine

"Outstanding...Embracing the *Pit of Success* is a liberating and empowering experience that produces results. I now have a set of principles to apply to any challenge no matter how difficult. Growth lies in the Pit!"

—**Thomas Walker**, Senior Director, eBay

"Incredible...really well written! You will be convinced that you have what it takes to overcome your challenges and doubts. *The Pit of Success* helps you improve quicker and with less stress. The tools enable you to embrace your temporary incompetence and elevate your confidence, results, and expertise. Applicable to all at whatever stage in life or career."

—**Jenn Watt**, Principal Talent Manager, Fortune 100 Company

"Highly recommend to anyone who needs to be reenergized on their personal or professional journey. *The Pit of Success* is full of useful tips and colorful stories that will help you no matter which side of the pit you find yourself on."

—**Frank Maylett**, Chief Revenue Officer, Instructure

"*The Pit of Success* gives leaders and their teams what they need to grow faster. I have personally experienced how the tools and concepts help push teams through their pit of success to become more aligned and strategic."

—**Garry Wiseman**, Chief Digital Officer, Nautilus

"If you are going through change or want to evolve to the next stage of your career, *The Pit of Success* provides great insights and confidence builders to help you achieve your goals. Jennings and Leishman's ability to see through change and help others succeed is powerful."

—**Josh Baxter**, CEO, NetDocuments

"Nicely done! The Pit of Success normalizes that all of the emotions of being out of your element are not only natural, but essential to truly transforming and moving ahead in your leadership, creativity, and outlook. The stories and guidance form a relatable and accessible way for leaders to trade up through the challenges of life and career."

—**Casey Cerretani**, General Manager, Microsoft Azure

"Important and very practical for both personal growth and work."

—**Carol Sato**, Vice President, Fortune 100 Company

"Powerful...Whether you're looking to live or lead at the next level, *The Pit of Success* delivers."

—**Chris Deaver**, Sr Director of HR
and Leadership Coach, VMWare

THE PIT OF SUCCESS

How Leaders Adapt, Succeed, & Repeat

DAVE
JENNINGS

AMY
LEISHMAN

NEW YORK

LONDON • NASHVILLE • MELBOURNE • VANCOUVER

The Pit of Success

How Leaders Adapt, Succeed, & Repeat

Published in New York, New York, by Morgan James Publishing. Morgan James is a trademark of Morgan James, LLC. www.MorganJamesPublishing.com

ISBN 9781631953828 paperback
ISBN 9781631953835 eBook
Library of Congress Control Number: 2020948944

Cover Design by:
Jamie Wright

Interior Design by:
Christopher Kirk
www.GFSstudio.com

Morgan James is a proud partner of Habitat for Humanity Peninsula and Greater Williamsburg. Partners in building since 2006.

Get involved today! Visit
MorganJamesPublishing.com/giving-back

Contents

Preface

As we teach leaders around the world about the *Pit of Success*, they continually tell us, "I wish I had known about this sooner." Whether they are a new leader, a stalled leader, or an executive with expanding responsibilities, they share this sentiment because when they understand the pit of success, they see themselves and their challenges in a whole new light.

These leaders are experiencing promotions, organizational changes, shifting markets, the need for new skills, new cultures, career changes, and personal crises that push them beyond their own expertise. As they begin to understand the pit of success, they increase their trust in themselves to conquer their challenges and to find greater meaning from those demands. They become more resilient at overcoming struggles.

We wrote this book to help leaders lighten the burdens they face as they grow throughout their careers. We wanted to enable leaders to take on progressively more demanding situations and come out on top. As leaders embrace the ideas behind the pit of success, their challenges become easier, their confidence grows, and their results improve.

Our research suggests that the steps you must take to cross the pit of success are learnable, even as you are tasked with learning increasingly difficult skills throughout your career. You never need to plateau or be stuck. You can keep getting better and better.

Welcome to *The Pit of Success: How Leaders Adapt, Succeed, and Repeat*. Your path is about to become clearer, and your ability to achieve greater.

PART ONE:

WHAT YOU NEED IS LEARNABLE

CHAPTER 1

Introduction: Navigating the Pit of Success

S tephanie Shirley did not intend to become a pioneer in computing. She just liked math and was fascinated with computers in the 1950s. While attending night school, she worked days for the United Kingdom's Post Office Research Station, assembling room-sized computers and teaching herself machine language programming. After graduating and working at a second firm, she decided it was time to start her own one-person programming company.

Stephanie gradually won programming contracts, including some that were beyond her level of experience, but the challenge never intimidated her, because she knew she had the talent and work ethic to solve any technical problem. She felt good about her success that first year until she received her tax returns and realized she was not getting ahead. She decided that she needed to build a scalable company, and with only £6 (approximately US$50 adjusted for inflation) of capital, she started the software company Freelance Programmers in 1962.

Stephanie could figure out how to program almost anything and worked hard to secure new projects, but she did not understand employee contracts, managing people, and cash-flow management. In her own words, "I didn't even know the issues existed, let alone that I needed to master them." Running a business was the first time that Stephanie felt in over her head. Despite her intelligence, optimism, and willingness to work hard, as her company grew, she was lost and floundering.

Stephanie often found herself being pulled away from doing what she loved—programming—to do the things she considered to be just "a headache," namely, leading the business. She soon had so many problems with overseeing quality, attending key meetings, and managing work deadlines that after only two years, she was on the brink of having to shut down Freelance Programmers. She was having serious doubts about her ability to succeed as the leader of a company.

Stephanie Shirley had entered what we describe as a *Pit of Success*. That is, she stood at a turning point between what had made her good up until then and what would make her good in the future. In her case, she needed to choose between being an excellent programmer and an effective leader.

Stephanie chose to lead and focused on learning how to manage people and understand business logistics. She gained some knowledge by taking classes, and she sought guidance from experts in the field to learn what it meant to lead a business. The company slowly began to turn around, and in the next three years, her company started becoming profitable. Moreover, Stephanie was feeling more comfortable as a leader.

With her newly acquired abilities, Stephanie continued to win contracts, create standardization for quality control, and expand her business. By 1980, she had grown the company to six hundred employees, and by 1987, some 25 percent of the top five hundred companies in the United Kingdom were her clients. Stephanie's willingness to navigate her pit of success, including her struggle to create standardization for her programming teams, resulted in the standards still used today by the North Atlantic Treaty Organization (NATO) to regulate software.

She has been honored many times for her pioneering work in information technology, including becoming a Fellow of the Royal Academy of Engineering. In 2000, she was given the honor of Dame Commander of the Order of the British Empire (the equivalent of knighthood) for her contributions to computing.

Dame Stephanie Shirley retired at the age of sixty in 1993 and since then has donated £67 million (approximately US$87 million) of her personal wealth to philanthropic projects around the world. She continues to this day to give her time and money to worthy causes.

To achieve her success, Dame Stephanie Shirley had to take herself and her business through the pit of success.

Leaders Achieve with Their Doubts

In our interviews with Fortune 500 executives, new managers, mid-managers, doctors, parents, community leaders, and politicians, we have found that Stephanie's struggles and doubts are shared by people in all walks of life and at all levels of leadership. And the reason is quite simple: the problems leaders face are routinely bigger than their experience. These challenges are the norm! Leaders are not in their jobs because they have all the answers to the problems. They are in their jobs to find answers.

Executives, parents, and other leaders routinely feel lost, confused, and overwhelmed as they try to find answers. Some leaders worry that they really are not up to the challenge. When they look around at others who seem so competent, they secretly wonder if they are alone in their struggles, and they wish they could keep doing what made them successful in the past.

Few leaders talk about these doubts because it does not seem "leader-like" to feel this way. Yet, no one is protected from these doubts. Your age, education, intelligence, gender, experience, position, or geography afford no safeguard from these uncertainties. When you face something bigger than your experience, you often feel doubt and confusion. In fact, uncertainty is one of the most common experiences shared by leaders across the planet. At some point, every leader faces a pit of success and wonders, "Am I good enough?"

What Is a Pit of Success?

A *pit of success* is the space between your current expertise and your future expertise. A pit could be any challenge, demand, opportunity, or indignity that pushes you beyond your expertise. We call this space a *pit* because it is confusing and stressful. It creates a sense of loss, makes you feel inadequate, and rarely has a clear path forward. When you are in the pit, you frequently feel like a fake or an imposter.

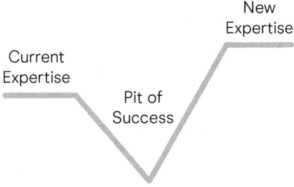

You may have a pit imposed on your life through organizational changes, job loss, difficult people, health problems, divorce, financial difficulties, depression, abuse, or other people's bad decisions. You did not seek these demands; nor did you deserve to have them come down on you. But you are stuck with them.

You may also have purposely chosen your pit of success, as Stephanie did. You might be seeking a promotion, taking on new responsibilities, pursuing a college class, starting a family, or learning a language. You believe these pits will make you better, so you seek them out, even though you know they will be demanding.

Either type of pit, imposed or chosen, can sometimes seem insurmountable. Imagining all the skills, interactions, decisions, and additional effort required to overcome it can be draining. Given the anticipated demands, you can easily begin to wonder how you will ever do it all.

These pits can make you feel that you should be better than you are. A pit can feel like a dark place with no exits—a place where you feel smaller than the task at hand. But being in a pit does not mean you are incapable; it only means you are unpracticed.

You transform your uncertainties into success when you redefine the pit. Rather than seeing it as something that minimizes you, you can redefine a pit as something that maximizes you—if you let it. By understanding how you progress from your current expertise through the pit and then to a new area of expertise, you can leverage a pit rather than avoiding or dreading it.

Enjoying Your Current Expertise

Your *current expertise* is the place where you perform certain tasks with ease. It is your mental home. You have worked hard and established a repertoire of skills, relationships, and knowledge through practice, trial and error, and study. When you are operating within an area of expertise and facing familiar challenges, it feels good. Your brain loves this space because it requires little effort. Familiar situations give you a sense of confidence.

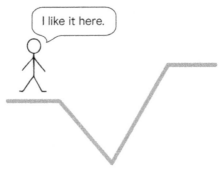

Being in your expertise zone does not mean you are perfect—or even the best at the task. It simply means you have mastered a set of knowledge, skills, routines, and beliefs that allow you to repeat your current level of success at will. There is a lot of comfort in your expertise zone.

When Stephanie Shirley began her company, her current expertise included the following capabilities:

- Knowledge of computers and programming
- The ability to learn new programming languages
- Experience solving complex technical problems
- The ability to obtain contracts
- Consistency in delivering her own projects

Staying within her current expertise provided Shirley with fun and rewarding work. Her strengths in understanding the problem, anticipating the process, and programming quality software gave her great satisfaction. She would have preferred to continue relying on her expertise to solve her new challenges.

Your current expertise may be quite different from Stephanie's, but the principle is the same. When you are in your current expertise, you feel confident. It is a place of strength. You know where things are, you know what needs to be done, and you know how to get things done. Here are a few typical ways you might experience your current expertise:

- Doing the work yourself
- Having a deep knowledge of a technology or process
- Predicting how long things will take to create
- Maintaining a network of stakeholders and colleagues
- Knowing a specific industry

When operating in your own area of expertise, you can predict success because you have been through this experience before. You know who to go to when you have a problem, and you can make timely decisions. This confidence allows you to move with ease. If the world never changed, your expertise would allow you to solve similar problems in the future.

But your current expertise is a bit of a paradox. On the one hand, your current skills, relationships, and mindset give you a foundation of strength for facing challenges. They give you power. These abilities protect you and give you competence to face the world.

On the other hand, the comfort of these strengths can also encourage you to avoid or even condemn unfamiliar and difficult demands. Because you invested heavily in your current expertise, the most natural thing to do is to rely on it, even when the situation no longer demands your strengths.

You do not cling to these strengths because you are lazy, stubborn, or stupid. You hold on to them because they have worked. They are the most natural response. But if left unchecked, your dependence on your current expertise will hold you back because it discourages you from discovering new and better approaches to problems. Managing this paradox helps you become more capable and resilient.

If Stephanie had insisted on sticking only with her current expertise, she could not have gained the skills she needed to lead a business. She had to overcome the paradox of her strengths and enter the pit.

Entering the Pit of Success

The pit of success begins with that "Oh no" moment when you realize that your current skills, knowledge, and relationships will not solve the problem in front of you. You look at the challenge and wonder, "How can I ever do it?" or, better yet, "How can I simply avoid it?" Moving forward into the pit means leaving your emotional and intellectual home. You stand between knowing how to do the old thing and learning the new thing. In essence, you are between two places you want to be.

Pits come in many different shapes and sizes:

- You know how to get the work done yourself, but now you must create a strategy that others will execute.
- You have technical expertise in one domain, but now you must learn a new domain.
- You know how to manage a team, but now you are managing an organization.
- You know how to succeed in a growing market, but now you must make a profit in a declining market.
- You know how to care for a young child, but now you must care for aging parents.

The emotions of entering the pit are like those of new trapeze artists when they must swing fifty feet above the ground, let go of the solid trapeze bar, and hope that, when they let go and turn around, the other trapeze bar will be there. As they anticipate letting go, they wonder, "Do I really want to let go of this bar? What if my timing is just slightly off? Am I strong enough to make the catch?" The fact that a net waits below does not eliminate the uncertainty. The artists cannot know if they will make it until they let go of the bar. It is a moment of fear—and possibly exhilaration.

In Stephanie's situation, not only did she have to let go of a bar that gave her great security and confidence, but she also had to make a huge stretch to catch a bar that was far away. She chose a new space requiring her to manage budgets, oversee the quality of others' work, and maintain cash flow, when she would have preferred to just keep programming and ignore the administrative details of the business.

Stephanie occasionally felt like an imposter as she tried to juggle her new world of management. Everything about running the business was a difficult decision for her because she could not rely on her experience to guide her actions. She had to think through everything, and it all took so much time. There were many days when Stephanie wished she could just go back to doing all the programming herself.

Like Stephanie, you may wish you did not have to let go of your current expertise to face your pit of success. That is a common feeling leaders experience as they try to navigate their existing world, where they feel confident, and their new world, where they do not have all the answers. In fact, reluctance to enter the pit is the norm.

As you struggle with your pit, you are likely to feel scared and even stupid. Many nagging thoughts may rise to the surface:

- "What was I thinking?!"
- "Why aren't I better at this? It is harder than I expected."
- "Do people know I am just faking it?"
- "I hope I don't make a fool of myself or hurt others."
- "Why are others so much better than I am?"

These doubts and other confusing emotions are the most common responses to a pit of success. Whether you are taking on a new job, changing roles, or learning a new skill, they are the most predictable responses you could have.

If you are willing to accept these feelings of inadequacy, doubt, and fear as a natural part of growth, you can spend each day of the rest of your life improving with less stress. However, if you routinely avoid situations where you feel lost, you will remain at your current level of expertise.

To sum up this idea, I (Dave) will use my daughter's words. She explained this dilemma the best when she came home from high school one day and exclaimed that she had finally gotten what I was trying to teach her: "If I am willing to feel stupid for a little bit, I can keep getting smarter and smarter." Exactly!

Your future depends on your willingness to be temporarily incompetent. If you are willing to *not* know how for a little while, accept imperfection as part of the process, and practice new ways of doing things, you can gain a whole new level confidence, results, and expertise.

Developing a New Expertise

Every new level of expertise has a pit of success in front of it, with varying depths and difficulty. At one time, your current level of expertise was beyond your earlier level. Riding a bike, talking to people, driving a car, passing a class, leading a meeting, giving a presentation, and running a computer were all once beyond your experience. Whether you are aware of it or not, you gained your current expertise by navigating many pits of

success, facing demands, handling ambiguities, learning hard things, and managing your doubts. You have already conquered many pits of success.

When Stephanie navigated her pit, she started where she was at and began learning new things, though she did them imperfectly. She struggled as a business leader when she started, but she learned how to run the business by gaining knowledge, making mistakes, letting go of some expertise, building relationships, seeking help, and moving forward. She became qualified by doing things beyond her experience and beyond her confidence level. There was no miracle cure. She had to navigate her own pit of success to make the business grow.

Organizations Succeed When Leaders Embrace the Pit

Organizations, like leaders, must also adapt and navigate the pit of success. Without leaders who are willing to enter the pit, organizations get stuck in patterns that generated yesterday's success, limiting their abilities to adapt to today's demands. Consider how two companies—and their leaders—faced the same pit differently.

Starting in 1985, Blockbuster Video became the leader in video rental, with millions of people visiting its stores each week. As DVDs displaced VHS (videos) as the norm for watching movies, distribution of DVDs through the mail became easy and cheap. No longer would a customer need to go to a store for a movie. In an attempt to stay competitive, Blockbuster began eliminating late fees and allowing customers to order DVDs online. But this act of progress was met with a lawsuit by Southern Stores Video, one of the largest Blockbuster franchise holders in the United States. Rather than seeing the changes as progress, the leader of the franchise, Fred Montesi III, saw them as a threat to his profits. Even though other leaders in Blockbuster could see the need for change, there were not enough leaders willing to embrace this pit of success to redirect the company in the midst of market pressures.

In contrast, Netflix was already sending out DVDs by mail. Seeing more technology advances on the horizon, the company believed that this market shift was an opportunity rather than a threat. It started the costly venture of investing in streaming movies. In embracing this change, Netflix leaders informed existing employees and new hires that their job of mailing out DVDs would steadily decline over the next three years and that they needed to either gain new skills or be prepared to find new work. The leaders of Netflix had made the changes within themselves about the future, and they were preparing their people to make the change. The costs and risks of walking away from the company's current expertise in providing DVDs were significant, but the leaders decided they needed to adapt.

In the year 2000, Blockbuster was offered—and rejected—an acquisition deal worth $50 million. In 2010, the company went bankrupt. In contrast, by 2020, Netflix was worth over $200 billion. As leaders from Netflix and Blockbuster looked at the same pit of success (a changing market), one group of leaders embraced the pit while the other avoided it.

Organizations Are Punished by Success

Why was it so hard for the largest Blockbuster franchisee to adapt? Organizations spend years developing their current expertise so that they can profitably create and distribute a product or service to customers. Because they are so good at their current expertise, customers reward the companies financially. Yet when demands change, many organizations will still rely on their existing expertise. They will try to polish what they have rather than taking on the difficult path of adapting.

Clayton Christensen called this tendency the *innovator's dilemma*. While an incumbent organization is busy succeeding with its current expertise, a new entrant comes to the market and creates a disruptive yet imperfect solution. It is not that the incumbent organization overlooks the need for the innovations. But rather that the organization has successes that it has worked hard for, and its customers reward the firm for its current strategy. For this reason, the organization finds it extremely hard to invest in unproven and riskier products. It wants to gain new expertise, but the opportunity costs are hard to justify and the sunk costs keep the organization from taking action.

Meanwhile, the new entrant is developing imperfect products to meet future customer needs. These imperfect solutions soon improve, and the customers find that they need the innovative product more than they need the incumbent's product.

The incumbent organization was punished by its own success. It focused so much on maximizing short-term profits that it ignored a changing market and held tight to its current expertise. Organizations—and more specifically, their leaders—must learn to manage this predicament to adapt and stay relevant.

Leaders Are Punished by Success

In assessing this dilemma, we can easily talk about how these organizations are just slow and out-of-date. But a more accurate description is that the *leaders* of these organizations are unable to adapt quickly enough—they are unwilling to enter the pit of success and gain new skills, knowledge, and insights. As Timothy Clark, founder and CEO of leadership consulting firm LeaderFactor, observes, "Organizations don't outperform their leaders; they reflect them."

While this description of leaders may sound critical, it not intended as an attack. It is simply a reality of life. Just like organizations, leaders are punished by their own success. Your brain gets wired to do certain things, so you do more of the same things. When you have a current expertise and you see the risks, unknowns, and time commitments of doing something new, you will tend to hold on to your existing expertise. This inclination is normal. Every leader faces the same dilemma: "Do I keep relying on my current expertise that has been rewarded, or do I start developing a new, unproven expertise?"

It is an incredibly difficult question to resolve, considering the time limitations, doubts, risks, and financial pressures staring you in the face. However, leaders can find ways to personally overcome this dilemma and help the people in their organization move toward new expertise. Organizations can more successfully adapt to changing markets as they support their leaders navigating the pit of success.

Navigating Your Pit of Success

A pit of success can be big or small, personal or organizational, imposed or chosen. There is no threshold to qualify for a pit of success. Whatever the challenge, if you have not done it, or something similar, it is your pit of success, and you do not automatically know how to get through it.

Fortunately, navigating your pit of success is learnable—no superpowers are required. You start where you are (genetics, predispositions, education, resources, and life experiences) and take the next step. It is truly a process of learning on the job.

Your ability to navigate the pit of success will be enhanced by practicing these five principles:

- **Hotwire your changeable brain:** Neuroscience provides undeniable proof that not only can your brain change and learn to navigate your pit of success, but also that you can start changing your brain and your results today. You are innately designed to adapt, and you can learn to change more effectively.

- **Embrace the pit:** While you cannot control what comes at you, you can control how you respond. Whether you chose your pit or it was imposed on you, you need not simply suffer through it and tolerate the experience. You can embrace your pit in a way that gives you more confidence and influence.

- **Trade up (and up):** Your brain can get stuck focusing on the wrong thing at the wrong time. And while your focus may have served you well in the past, it may not be useful for your current situation. As you trade up, you can focus on the right thing at the right time and reach your goals more quickly.

- **Make something from nothing:** Every demanding situation can make you feel trapped. However, there are always more options to resolve a problem than are initially obvious. Learning to find more options and innovate with what you have (or what you can create) gives you the power to solve challenges beyond your experience. As you expand your options, you will literally change the chemicals in your brain and increase your capabilities.

- **Slow down to speed up:** A pit of success can easily deplete you. But you can go faster with more strength when you slow down in brain-friendly ways. As you care for your brain, you will find that you can achieve peace, energy, speed, and greater results in the midst of your pit.

Any one of these principles will have a positive and significant impact on your career or life. Each principle is a resource, and different situations will ask you to draw on these resources. Sometimes, just one principle is more than enough to help you through a pit of success. Other times, a combination of principles is best. As you practice each principle, you will become better at the other principles.

Your ability to confidently navigate your pit of success starts with understanding your changeable brain. We will examine this skill in detail in the next chapter.

Key Ideas

- Leaders are not in their jobs because they have all the answers. They are in their jobs to find answers.
- Leaders can achieve great things even with their doubts.
- Your current expertise is like home, and it is normal to avoid entering the pit of success with all its attendant unknowns.
- When entering the pit of success, you feel like a fake. You doubt you are good enough, feel stressed, find it hard to make decisions, and want to go back to the familiarity of your expertise.
- Your growth depends on your willingness to be temporarily incompetent.
- Every new expertise has a pit of success in front of it.
- Organizations can suffer from the innovator's dilemma and be punished by their success.
- Organizations benefit from, or are limited by, their leaders' willingness or unwillingness to embrace the pit of success.
- As situations and markets change, you may be punished by your success and seek to hold on to your current expertise.
- Leaders need to answer these questions:
  - What is encouraging my business (or team) to hold on to its current expertise and to avoid the pit?
  - What is encouraging my business to embrace the pit?

- What is encouraging me to hold on to my current expertise?
- What pit should I personally embrace so that I can change the business or my team?

• You can navigate the pit easier when you practice these principles:

- Hotwire your changeable brain
- Embrace the pit
- Trade up (and up)
- Make something from nothing
- Slow down to speed up

CHAPTER 2

Hotwire Your Changeable Brain

S tanding in front of a stadium filled with over seventy-six thousand soccer fans, Juliano Pinto kicked the ceremonial opening ball at the World Cup held in Brazil in 2014. The ball traveled only a few feet before an official picked it up and carried it to the middle of the field to begin the game.

The crowd cheered the seemingly unimpressive kick, and Juliano raised one hand in victory, smiling as though he had made the winning goal. You see, Juliano is paralyzed below his neck. He has not stood and kicked a soccer ball in years.

The twenty-nine-year-old Juliano was one of eight paraplegics participating in the Walk Again Project jointly sponsored by Brazil University and Duke University to investigate the ability of paralyzed individuals to control a robotic exoskeleton with their mind. When Juliano signed up for the program, he did not know exactly what he was getting himself into. Maybe it would be a waste of time, he thought, but maybe there was a chance he could move again without a wheelchair.

Over several months, Juliano and seven other participants learned to mentally activate an exoskeleton that forced their legs to move. Their efforts brought many tearful moments of joy for researchers and participants alike. When Juliano stood with the assistance of the exoskeleton and kicked the ceremonial soccer ball, it was a symbolic moment of human progress.

Yet, incredibly, controlling the exoskeleton was not the real breakthrough of the study. After seven months of training to mentally move the robotic exoskeleton, Juliano did something more than move the exoskeleton—he actually moved his own legs without robotic help!

But wait, you might say, that is impossible. The medical community knows that in the case of paraplegia, once the nerves are damaged, they do not regenerate enough to allow movement like Juliano's. This was a groundbreaking result. It went beyond the limits of what scientists knew about neuroplasticity and nerve damage. What was "true" seven months ago was no longer true. As Juliano's brain repeatedly fired the neural pathways that caused him to move the exoskeleton, he inexplicably learned to move his legs. The brain created a new pathway, a feat that until now had been considered impossible.

What Is Impossible for You?

Many pits in life feel impossible to conquer. The current demands, past failures, unknowns, required effort, and doubts cloud your ability to know what can be achieved. Consequently, it can be easy to jump to self-defeating conclusions:

- It's just too hard for me.
- I'm too old (or too young) to change.

- I tried before and failed.
- I'm just not smart enough.
- It's impossible.

In these moments, you are unconsciously telling yourself, "My brain won't change." Or, more specifically, "I can't change." Whether you are fixing a leaky faucet, figuring out taxes, passing a big test, overcoming a betrayal, managing a health setback, helping your teenager, improving relationship issues, or taking on a leadership position, if you are unsure about your ability to do it, avoidance is a logical choice. However, when you better understand what your brain is capable of, you gain a new level of personal power.

Your Brain Changes: A Crash Course in Brain Science

If you ignore the billions of neural connections that must be navigated, the brain is remarkably simple. Change in a healthy brain comes down to a predictable cycle: whatever you focus on and repeat will lead to a change, a new habit, a new way of thinking, or a new skill.

Focus + Repetition → Change

Whether you are learning to play the piano, negotiate contracts, or make small talk, the brain responds to repetitive demand. What the brain does repeatedly, it gets better at doing—even if the behavior is bad for you or is the wrong way of doing it. Your brain chemistry and wiring do not discriminate about the goodness or badness of a repeated behavior. If you eat a bag of chips every day, your brain gets used to reaching for a bag of chips. If you eat an apple every day, your brain gets used to that. If you avoid an interaction, you train yourself to avoid it. If you say a certain phrase often, you say it even more often.

The frequency of repetition is important. If you practice once a year (the piano, your tennis backhand, or speaking up in a meeting), then you are not likely to develop the skill. The connection in the brain requires timely repetition to make the skill stick. If your skill is not improving, you may want to assess how long and how often you practice. Most skills require daily or weekly practice to see noticeable change.

(Note: Certain brain conditions reduce the brain's ability to learn but for neurotypical brains—that is, for most of the population—repetition creates predictable change and skill adoption.)

Physical Brain Changes

Using functional magnetic resonance imaging (fMRI) of people's brains, researchers have shown that repeated exercises (e.g., practicing an instrument, learning a new language) cause specific areas of the brain to change. Consider these studies:

- London taxi drivers were evaluated before and after their three months of preparation for their qualification exam. The fMRI showed increases in the size of brain areas related to spatial processing.
- Individuals with no experience juggling showed, after two weeks of practicing juggling, changes in the part of their brain related to motor skills.
- Individuals who learned braille showed changes in their occipital lobe, the part of the brain that controls visual activity.

The list of ways your brain physically changes could go on and on. The brain is proven to physically change with demand. The brain literally grows in the direction in which you focus.

In everyday terms, this means that every time you sit on the couch—instead of heading out for a walk—you increase your ability to sit on the couch until finally with enough repetition you actually achieve Olympic-level couch-sitting ability. However, if you repeat going for a walk—instead of sitting "just for a minute"—you will eventually get better at taking time to walk until it becomes your preferred choice. The change is not merely dependent on willpower; it is neuroscience. In fact, much of what we criticize ourselves over has little to do with willpower but more to do with how much (or how little) we have exercised the brain in the direction we want to go.

Ways the Brain Changes
Beyond the physical changes that occur within the brain, there are pragmatic results that come from these changes. Here is a sample of just three amazing ways the brain can change and achieve results when the brain is refocused.

Scenario 1: Defying Age
Michael Merzenich, a neuroscientist professor and a pioneer of modern brain science, wanted to determine if age really prevented people from learning and changing. He provided a group of eighty- to ninety-year-old men and women thirty hours of brain training, and the results were astounding. These older adults made statistically significant improvements in memory, cognition, attention, and visual spatial abilities. After just thirty hours, their abilities improved by two standard deviations. That means that if they were doing

poorly before the training, they achieved at least average performance after the training. And if they were performing at an average level beforehand, they were now performing at an advanced level. Our judgments about aging and the brain are out-of-date; being old does not mean you cannot learn. The brain is still adaptable. The areas in the brain that are stimulated by repetition continue to grow.

Scenario 2: Making Healthy the Priority

A research team in London wanted to determine if a person's typical response to sweets could be reprogramed to choose healthy foods over unhealthy. To do this, a group of "normal" unhealthy eaters was given fMRIs to determine a baseline of their brain's activity as it was exposed to the different foods. As expected, the sweets excited the brain more than healthy foods did.

However, after the participants received six months of training in healthy diet and exercise, fMRIs revealed changes in the brain, specifically in its reward center associated with learning and addiction. This area increased its sensitivity to healthy, lower-caloric foods. In other words, the brain got excited when seeing vegetables but less excited when seeing a candy bar. The brain learned to respond differently.

Scenario 3: Applying an Incremental Mindset to Hard Things

Carol Dweck, a professor of psychology at Stanford University, conducted research with children of similar cognitive abilities to evaluate how they would respond to difficult problems beyond their experience. The children fell into two groups: children with a fixed definition of their intelligence (the abilities they have now are all they will ever have) and those with an incremental definition of their intelligence (their abilities and intelligence can increase with effort).

Dweck found that those in the fixed-mindset group condemned the problem, defined themselves as incapable, and quickly quit trying. The kids with an incremental mindset, however, defined the problem in positive ways, looked for new strategies or skills to solve the problem, and kept working long after the others had quit. The incremental-mindset group significantly outperformed the fixed-mindset group.

Dweck's team then went into a school and taught underperforming five-year-old children to think with an incremental mindset (later known as a *growth mindset*). During one school year, these kids moved from the lowest performers to achieving in the 95th percentile of their school district. Similar studies have been repeated for different ages, socioeconomic levels, and geographic locations, but the results have been consistent. Children who were low performing improved significantly when they came to believe that their brain was malleable and that they could grow into their challenge.

Your Brain, the Pits, and Adapting

These examples about the brain illustrate the same story. Whether it is learning a skill, adapting to structural changes, or seeing the world differently, the brain is resilient and can be rewired. You have the innate ability to rewire the connections in your brain so that you can manage the pit of success in front to you. Whether you are facing a new job, a new boss, a new industry, a new product, an expanded scope, a new culture, or a difficult relationship, your brain can rewire and you can become more capable.

Your Learning Curve

The science is clear: your brain changes with repetition. With practice, your brain will gradually rewire until you have that "click" moment and you can do the new task with ease. The speed at which you get your brain to change is known as the *learning curve*; your curve will differ according to your experiences with the task, your genetics, how frequently your brain does the task, and complexity of the task.

Different Speeds, Same Mastery

The time it takes for your brain to make a new pathway does not predict whether you will master a task in the long term. Once your brain fully makes the connection, you have mastery. It does not matter how long it takes you to learn the task. You gain mastery at your own speed. When the connection is made, you have mastery!

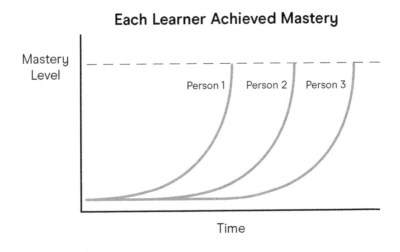

For example, young preschoolers and kindergarteners learning to read will master the alphabet at different rates. Some master it with just a few repetitions, while others take more time and may need added resources to support their learning. But the outcome is the same: the students master the alphabet and then move to the more complex tasks involved in reading. Likewise, mastering a skill required for your pit of success may take longer or shorter, but once the path is made in your brain, you have gained mastery of that skill.

One major factor in how fast you learn is your familiarity with the skill. For example, the following skills are easier to learn under certain conditions:

- Learning French when your native language is Italian
- Starting the same type of job at a new company when the position is in the same industry
- Learning cello when you already play the violin

In each of these examples, you have something to draw on that makes the new skill easier. The existing neural pathways provide a foundation for building the new skill, and you are not mentally taxed with learning as much.

In contrast, when you lack a similar foundation for the new task, it just takes longer to make the connection. You have fewer existing pathways for you brain to use. For example, the following situations would make learning a skill slower or more difficult:

- Learning French when your native language is Chinese
- Succeeding at a new job in a totally different industry
- Learning to play drums when you have only played the violin

Fortunately, in both familiar and unfamiliar situations, your brain will adapt and learn with practice. Your progress on the learning curve may take you five tries, fifteen, or fifty. No one knows when your brain will make the connections you need, but your brain will make the connection with repetition.

If you are not mastering a skill as quickly or as easily as you would like, you do not need to blame the difficulty on your willpower, your goodness, your character, or your smarts. Your brain has simply not repeated the action enough to make a clear neural pathway. That is all. Once your brain rewires itself, however, you can perform the new behavior just as well as someone who got it quicker can perform it. Your brain will be rewired with repetition, and you will have mastery of that skill.

You Should NOT Be Better Yet

When you are attempting to conquer a new pit—and trying to get your brain to respond in a new way—you may have plenty of doubts:

- Why aren't I getting this faster?
- Others are getting this. What's wrong with me?
- Shouldn't I be better at this?

These concerns that you should be better may be well intentioned, but they limit your ability to learn. When you assume a predefined learning curve and condemn yourself for not meeting this imaginary bar, you—in addition to being miserable—are likely to give up too early.

For example, master chess players can play multiple games of chess simultaneously. They go from board to board and move the chess pieces effortlessly, often moving a piece in less than a second while their novice opponent sits and thinks and thinks about the next move. If you were that novice, you might condemn your abilities and believe you should better. In addition, you may be tempted to proclaim the brilliance of your opponent and the inferiority of yourself. These master players, however, have worked hours and hours to memorize thousands of board layouts, and they already have an answer that they know works. They are not thinking deeply as they go from board to board but are recalling an established pattern in their brain. They are not on a learning curve when they are playing against you. They already know what to do because they have worked at it. Simply calling them brilliant discounts the price they paid to wire their brain for chess.

Whether you are playing chess against one of these masters or facing another pit of success, there is no reason you should be better than you are right now. Your brain has not faced this challenge before. It has not practiced the moves. But you can learn the same patterns that the masters know, and then you can respond more easily to your pit. For now, with this new challenge, you cannot expect instant mastery.

Your Brain Needs the Building Blocks

In the 1960s, researchers were interested in understanding whether kids who were getting lower grades were merely incapable or if something else was at play. The researchers found that when the learning approach changed, the children's performance improved.

For example, in various studies during this period, the researchers discovered that the problem was not the children's lack of ability. Instead, the students were missing a key piece of knowledge needed to master the concept—they were missing a building block. When the researchers identified the missing building block and trained the students to master this building block of knowledge, the number of children receiving an A grew from a select few to 80 to 98 percent of all students. Thus, the ability to learn was based not on how "smart" the students were but on their grasp of the building blocks. With the right feedback, a full understanding of the concepts, and practice, these students were able to excel. Rather than being left behind because they missed a building block, these students gained mastery over that skill when their learning curve changed. The researchers identified what was missing, and the teachers guided the students to learn these missing elements.

To put this in perspective, imagine a construction company building a bridge that cars will cross for many years. But during construction, one of the metal support beams was not delivered.

Can you imagine just pushing forward without the beam? Of course not. No reputable construction company would dream of leaving out that support beam or just sticking in any old piece of wood and hoping for the best. The builders would invest the time and money to obtain the steel beam. They would measure what was needed, order it, obtain the supplies to install it, and, finally, put the support beam in place. And if the company needed extra time or help to accomplish these tasks, it would not hesitate to reach out. No one would question the company's taking the time to install the steel support beam properly.

Your situation is no different from that facing the bridge builder. You need support beams to build your future and navigate your pit. If you are not getting a skill, it does not mean you are incapable. It only means you are missing a building block needed to reach the next level. You have to pause and take the time to find and build the skill (for more on this step, see Appendix B, "Identifying Your Building Blocks").

When you stop looking at the speed of your learning curve and start looking at the building block you need, a unique phenomenon happens: you will achieve more at a faster rate. A lack of a current ability is not the predictor of your future but is just a sign that something is missing. As you realize you are merely missing a building block, judgments and self-condemnation fade away and freedom and confidence increase. You have a brain that can learn the next building block.

No, You Cannot Just Skip the Curve

If you are like most people, you would probably love to skip the learning curve. You want to be good at piano, leadership, conversation, communications, or cooking right away, with very little work. You may even subconsciously say to yourself: "I don't want to have to practice. I don't want to feel incompetent. I don't want to put out effort anymore. I want the laws of brain science and learning to be changed for me. I just want to be good now."

These thoughts are a normal response. Unfortunately, your desire to avoid the curve does not change the learning process. You must focus and repeat until your brain creates a new path and performs the task naturally. Currently, your brain is prepared to do what it has already done. But your brain is also ready and willing to learn what is next. You have what it takes to hotwire your brain to make it through your pit of success.

How to Start Hotwiring Your Brain

Your brain is ready to get started. In as few as three attempts of repeating a behavior, your neural circuitry begins to form a new path. With practice, you can make permanent connections that give you the skills you need.

You can start hotwiring your brain with these three approaches: beliefs, words, and actions.

Beliefs: Assess Your Belief in Your Changeable Brain

Studies have shown that when people define their brains as capable of changing, problems are easier to solve. Asking yourself just how much you believe your brain can adapt is the first acceleration point for taking advantage of your innate abilities.

You do not have to have a perfect knowledge of, or belief in, your brain's ability to change to see improvement; every little bit helps. In one study, merely reading a paragraph about the changeable nature of the brain shifted how participants approached the problems they encountered. They did not have to fully believe the paragraph they had read, but merely reading about the brain's changeable nature altered their approach to a problem. In fact, just considering the possibility that your brain can change will alter your brain chemicals and increase your ability to solve problems. By reading the studies in this chapter, it is likely that you have already started hotwiring your brain to be more capable of adapting and learning.

One man who never gave up on his brain's ability to change is George Dawson. George lived ninety-eight years without the ability to read. His illiteracy caused him to be tricked by an early employer, lose track of his parents because of his inability to read the mail, and fake many interactions that required reading. He lived a humble life working on a dairy farm until he retired.

George had wanted to read his whole life but was always afraid to reveal that he was illiterate. However, on meeting retired teacher Carl Henry, the ninety-eight-year-old started practicing reading with the belief that his brain could change. Within a year, he achieved his goal: literacy. George's confidence that his brain could still change gave him the motivation to learn to read. He continued to believe in his changeable brain and wrote an autobiography that was published just two years after he started learning to read.

George could have looked at his ninety-eight years of illiteracy and decided that this reading skill could not be mastered, but he believed differently. His brain, like that of the many other older adults around the world who have learned to read late in life, retained the ability to be rewired.

Hopefully, you are sold on the idea that your brain is changeable. But if you and your brain need a nudge, just ask yourself, "What would I do if I thought my brain really could change?" Just considering the question increases your ability to find answers and solve problems.

Words: Choose Brain-Friendly Words

Your brain cares about the words you use to describe your situation. When you define a pit of success as a "pit of despair," "unfair," "an enemy," or "impossible," or when you define yourself as incapable, small, or undeserving, your brain heads into a fight, flight, or freeze mindset. Simply thinking to yourself, "No, no, no, I don't have what it takes," triggers activity in your amygdala (the part of your brain involved in processing emotions) and starts sending stress chemicals into the rest of your body.

Researchers Andrew Newberg and Mark Waldman have shown that your brain's response to different words can be detected with fMRI scans. Using words like *helpless, impossible, unfair, stupid, beyond me,* or *incapable* to define your situation can send your amygdala into overdrive, essentially leaving your brain feeling overwhelmed and stuck.

Fortunately, you can interrupt these signals by choosing different words when you face a pit. As you choose more pragmatic words and phrases, your brain's response shifts to a problem-solving mode and seeks to find answers, instead of fixating on obstacles.

Old Description → New Description

Old Description	New Description
• I'm incapable.	• This is difficult. I'll need practice.
• I'm not good enough.	• I don't have this *yet!* I wonder what will help.
• I should be faster/better.	• What *can* I control or influence?
• This is impossible.	• What are smaller steps?
	• This is all new to me. I wonder who can help me see this better.

Note that *none* of these new descriptions were "positivity" statements (I'm awesome, I'm invincible, etc.). This change in language is not intended to merely make you feel more positive but rather to make your words more useful and accurate. Your brain likes high-quality information that directs you in the way you want to go.

Actions: Start with Starting

Sometimes a pit of success seems insurmountable. Imagining all the skills, effort, interactions, and decisions required to overcome a challenge can make you stand and stare into space—or walk the other way. Getting started in small ways is key, and the brain science supports this approach.

Small actions create energy, and those actions do not have to be perfect. An imperfect first attempt is better than ruminating endlessly on a flawless path. Some things you must do poorly before you can do them well. You cannot speak a new language without saying phrases with an improper accent at first. You cannot play violin without a few screeches. Nor can you lead your first meeting without a few detours. You cannot learn a skill perfectly without getting some feedback regarding what is working and what is not.

Phrases like the following can help get you started on the next thing:

- What is the simplest (or smallest) next thing I can do?
- I can't do ___, but I can do ___. (For example, "I can't put an hour into this task, but I can give it five minutes.")
- Who can give me helpful advice?

You do not need perfect answers to start your journey. You simply have to take the next small step, and your brain's ability to learn will do the rest.

Your Brain Can Keep Learning

When the eight participants started the earlier-mentioned Walk Again Project, they did not know what was possible or if the research was worth the effort. Their paralyzed bodies gave them lots of reason to doubt. Yet, Juliano and his colleagues progressed so significantly that 50 percent of the participants were reclassified from completely paralyzed to only partially paralyzed, and, remarkably, all the participants experienced voluntary movement and feeling in their legs.

What is fully possible for you—and your brain—in the challenges you must face is yet to be discovered. If you lack an ability that you need, it simply means that you have not found the building blocks and practiced them enough to achieve what you want. But one thing is for sure: your changeable brain can navigate your pit of success and learn more things than you could have ever imagined.

Key Ideas

- You have a changeable brain that can be rewired. It is just simple neuroscience. Focus plus timely repetition creates new abilities.

- When you recognize that your brain is incrementally changeable, you are more likely to behave in ways that will give you success. In other words, when you believe that your efforts can affect your intelligence, aptitude, and outcomes, you are more likely to succeed than when you believe that your current proficiencies cannot be changed.

- It may take you more or less time than others take to learn something new, but learning is not a competition. Your learning curve is *your own* learning curve. Once you acquire the skill, you have mastery, no matter how slowly or quickly you obtained it.

- You can make the path less difficult by reducing unhealthy *should*s. You are where you are, and success starts where you are. You may not succeed today. But with practice, your brain can make the connections and you can gain a skill or figure out a solution tomorrow.

- If you are not learning something in a timely manner, find the missing building block and seek expert advice.

- You may feel exhausted when you are doing new things because your brain is literally working harder. It is struggling to make a pathway, and this effort can create discomfort and fatigue. No one is exempt from the learning curve.

- Your brain is more capable of solving problems when you recognize that it is malleable, when you choose brain-friendly words, and when you take small steps.
- A company is a collection of people, all of whom have changeable brains. The more that people internalize this changeability, the easier it is for an organization to adapt to evolving market needs. Leaders must help their people discover their changeable brains.
- You have what it takes to conquer your pit of success. You may simply need some practice.

The Changeable Brain Is a Tool, Not a Weapon

It can be tempting to weaponize the idea of a changeable brain against yourself (or others) and assume that perfection is the only acceptable path forward. You may assume that all you or others need to do is blissfully remember your brain's abilities and your woes all go away.

This view is an incomplete picture, however. We all experience times of sadness, loss, regret, and painful mistakes. It is rarely helpful to tell ourselves (or others), "You should just get over it. You have a changeable brain, and you will grow from this." Expecting everything to fall in line because you can grow and learn ignores moments of the heart.

Understanding that you have a changeable brain does not eliminate the heartbreaks and doubts, but it can reduce the depth and duration of the struggle.

CHAPTER 3

Embrace the Pit

B randon (not his real name) graduated from a top MBA school, where he had been on the honor role, run the student investment portfolio, and completed an internship with a Fortune 500 company. Because of the turbulent market at the time of his graduation, the company instituted a hiring freeze just before he would have been eligible for a job offer.

Undeterred, Brandon aggressively networked and in a couple of months got an offer from a premier consulting firm that gave him even more opportunities than the previous company would have provided. His five years of experience in the financial world before his MBA made him qualified to start in a higher-level consulting role than the roles assigned to most new MBAs, and given his experience, the company was already discussing the probability of promotion to manager in a year.

Brandon was excited to land such a cool consulting job that could take advantage of his skills, keep him growing, and provide promotional opportunities. He was immediately assigned to a client project with six experienced consultants. He looked forward to learning from the team members as well as showcasing his own abilities.

But the work was more difficult than he had imagined, and he had to spend more time learning the basics than he had expected. He often felt lost in some meetings and was not sure if he should take the manager's time by asking questions.

He was shocked to feel so overwhelmed and stupid. He was not used to feeling this way and could not believe he was not getting things faster. To make things worse, he could not figure out if he was doing the wrong things or simply doing the right things poorly. Brandon lamented, "I thought I would be so much better."

Different Pits, Same Hard Things

When you choose a pit of success, as Brandon did, you do so because you want to grow and achieve something special. Similarly, when you seek a promotion, pursue a college degree, learn a new skill, change locations, or grow your family, you are moving toward that pit because of what it can give you. It provides you with a desirable difficulty—a difficulty with a purpose and a result that can benefit you or others. These pits can seem purposeful and inspiring from the start, even though they are hard and might make you feel stupid.

In contrast, when a pit is imposed on you by forces outside your choosing—your manager, market demands, losing your job, nature, other people's actions, or your own missteps—you typically face the challenge with no interest in growing. Juliano did not choose to be paralyzed. His pit did not come with a special noble feeling of growth. Imposed pits are often unwanted and devoid of initial meaning.

On the surface, imposed pits of success may appear vastly different from chosen ones. But both imposed and chosen pits push you to do things beyond your experience. Although a chosen pit initially gives you positive momentum, that advantage dissipates as you struggle to do things you do not know how to do. Both chosen and imposed pits are full of hard things that make you doubt yourself and make you want to avoid the pain.

Avoiding the Pit Is Natural

Avoiding the difficulties of a pit of success is one of the most natural first responses you can have to a demand. It is perfectly normal to protect yourself from potential mistakes, embarrassment, doubt, and other unwanted feelings. The things you avoid reveal what you care about and what you fear.

You Are Not Stupid

Of course, you want to avoid unnecessary pain and effort. After all, you are not stupid. You do not like doing things that may hurt you, waste your time, require too much effort, make you look bad, or have unpredictable outcomes. People naturally have a protective response in unfamiliar or overwhelming situations. If you embraced every pit that came your way, you would be a mess and accomplish little or nothing.

The dilemma is not your desire to protect yourself from pain. Rather, it is knowing when to stop protecting yourself by relying on your past expertise. People's brains have a hard time believing that what worked in the past does not work anymore, even though circumstances have changed.

Leaving Your Expertise Is Hard for Your Brain

While part of this response can be explained by the brain's desire to do what it already knows how to do, another part of the problem is that your brain can get confused and make you think you are winning when you are not. Kyle Siler at Cornell University has studied more than twenty-seven million online winning and losing poker hands to predict what gamblers are likely to do in different scenarios. His studies have shown that players give significantly more credit to small and near wins while minimizing the pain of their losses. In other words, the more the players have made a bet and come close to winning, the more likely they are to do it again—*even if it is not paying off.* The brain is seeing near wins (losses) as encouragement. It sees the last hand as having more influence on the future than is possible in any game of chance. And thus, the gambler places another bet instead of walking away.

We often place bets on behaviors that have served us well in the past and discount the losses those actions are giving us. We assume that this habit will soon pay off if we just keep playing it. In our brain, the habit feels like a safe bet. Thus, we avoid embracing the pit in front of us and we keep doing what we know.

Here are some signs that you are avoiding a pit:

- Blaming others
- Condemning yourself
- Repeating old behaviors
- Ignoring feedback
- Pushing away help
- Demanding how things "should" be
- Withdrawing or hiding
- Discounting information
- Assuming everything is out of your control

As described earlier, when Stephanie Shirley was running her software startup in the 1960s, she wanted to maintain her hands-on involvement rather than take care of the business itself. She liked sticking to what she knew—a normal response—even though this behavior was not helping her or her company advance.

You cannot really blame Stephanie for wanting to do programming-related work. You need to blame her brain. Given a choice between greater effort for unfamiliar, unknown rewards and doing what your brain already knows how to do, your brain will usually go on autopilot to the comfort of its existing expertise. Your brain is wired to repeat and will keep repeating a pathway unless you intentionally interrupt it and embrace the new demand—whether the demand was chosen or imposed.

Pragmatism, Not Optimism

Embracing the pit does not mean you must love, like, want, or need what has happened to you. In fact, you may hate what you have been given. It could be completely unfair that this pit stands in front of you.

However, what brought you the pit and what you do with it are two very different issues. You can condemn the source of the pit and still embrace what needs to be done.

The goal of embracing the pit is to gain the maximum benefit from what you have been given. Sometimes that benefit is for you, and other times you embrace the pit because it helps others. In either case, you will want to use the pit to your greatest advantage. Whether it is a promotion, a job loss, a new skill, a terrible boss, a difficult colleague, or a wayward child, the goal is to get the most from the situation.

You do not need to be naive or overly optimistic to make a pit work to your advantage. Embracing the challenge is about being pragmatic.

Five Approaches to Embracing the Pit

While dismay might be your first response to a pit, it does not have to be your permanent state of mind. Embracing the pit is about creating a new habit of mind so that you can move quickly from "Oh no, why me?" to "Oh wow! How can I use this challenge?" Embracing adversity, just like any other skill, is learned with practice.

These five approaches make it easier to embrace your pit:

- Find a why.
- Redefine the betweenness.
- Focus on discovery.
- Narrow your scope.
- Ask for advice and feedback.

As you review these approaches, we recommend that you do not worry about doing them all at once. Each approach has a time and place that can work for you. Start with one tactic that seems appropriate, and try another one later.

Find a Why

A pit is easier when you find a good reason to face the demands. Individuals who find a why—a clear purpose for doing something—have been shown to be more successful at work, community, education, health, and social settings. Angela Duckworth, author of *Grit,* found in her research that individuals with higher scores on measures of purpose also showed higher scores on the Grit Scale and concluded that these individuals show more motivation to persevere through challenges.

Clarifying your purpose has been correlated with several benefits:

- Giving meaning to the challenges or obstacles and making them worth your effort
- Believing that your actions will influence your outcomes (a mindset correlated with more goal-centered actions and positive results)
- Reducing the perceived difficulty of the struggle

Purpose gives you a reason to put up with the doubts, extra effort, risks, demands, unfairness, and confusion that can exist in a pit of success. It allows you to look beyond the moment and see something more than the current difficulty.

A Personal Why

I (Dave) had a personal experience in which a sense of purpose allowed me to do something that I absolutely wanted to avoid. When my then sixteen-year-old son became interested in rock climbing, I decided that a good way to connect with him was to join him in the adventure. There was one major problem: I am terribly afraid of falling! This fear is so great that if I just think about being next to the edge of a building or cliff, my body fills with panic. In fact, even if I see someone else next to the edge, I feel the same fear.

Because of my desire to connect with my son, however, I took lessons and signed up for climbing excursions with him. We worked together in the indoor gym, climbed 100-foot rock spires in national parks, and ascended the face of a sheer mountain with nothing more than a rope and a thin crack in the mountain to stick our fingers into. As I would attempt these climbs, the feeling was always the same: fear. But the fear was worth it to me. My son was happy and excited to climb, and I got quality time with my son.

To this day, I do not seek out climbing, but I would do it all again. When you find something that matters to you, it is easier to embrace the pit.

Purpose comes in all shapes and sizes. Some seem quite big and noble, while others seem more routine. Although your personal why may be great or magnanimous, you do not always require a grand purpose to get the meaning, direction, and energy you need to manage your pit of success.

Here are a few of the many purposes people find for embracing a pit of success:

- Achieving a goal
- Providing for others
- Graduating
- Influencing direction
- Building relationships
- Caring for a child or parent
- Developing a skill
- Paying the mortgage
- Giving encouragement
- Living with integrity

There is no one magical why; your own purpose reflects what is important to you. A first step in reconnecting with your purpose is to ask yourself several questions:

- Why is this struggle important to me?
- How can I use the demand to benefit myself or others?
- What matters more than the difficulty and doubts that this pit engenders?
- What is my new job description? What are the new expectations? How will I measure success in this role? Why does this role matter? How do I want to add value?

Remembering your existing purpose or creating a new one will give you the strength and hope to more easily embrace a pit of success.

A Business Why

Clarifying purpose applies at both personal and business levels. As you establish a compelling organizational why, it will become easier for you and others to see the pit as worth embracing. The goal of an organizational why is not to have a pretty statement hanging on the wall but rather to establish a practical guide for decisions and actions. While not everyone will care equally about the organizational purpose, the lack of a clear one will surely amplify individual doubts. A strong organizational purpose can increase individuals' ability to make decisions, focus their efforts, and prioritize effectively.

Redefine the Betweenness

The pit can make you feel as if you are nowhere. You are no longer standing firmly as an expert, where you feel at home, and you are not yet capable of the skills needed to perform at a new level. You are simultaneously disconnected from the past and not a part of the future.

This moment can translate into a time of exhaustion and uncertainty. Wanting to escape the nowhere and nothingness is a natural initial response. After all, this undefined state can make you feel as though you are not supposed to be there and that this space is your enemy.

But rather than condemning the in-between space, you can leverage it by redefining it. When you define the *betweenness* as a place you are supposed to be, a place where you belong, you are better able to embrace the pit and use the experience. To redefine this state of betweenness, keep in mind the following observations:

- The in-between space is not a *nowhere* but is a very definite *somewhere* that exists between other spaces.
- It is normal to encounter betweenness through all changes of life. You are not in this undefined space as some kind of punishment. You are between places because you are about to create something new.

- The in-between space is crucial for facilitating change. Without this moment of betweenness, there is no next level. Every sunrise must have a dawn. The betweenness is the needed transition that leads to your next great success.
- When you label the in-between state as its own space, you give yourself permission to experience it as it is. When you say, "I am between," you suddenly find that you are actually on solid ground and that you are where you should be, despite not knowing exactly what to do next.

To be in a pit is to be between two stages in your professional or personal life. Redefining the betweenness as a real and important place gives you freedom to be there without judgment or expectations. You are free to experience, learn, and grow, with betweenness as your ally.

Focus on Discovery

Embracing a pit of success is easier when you define missteps and detours as *steps* in the process of discovery, rather than mistakes. If you define each misstep as a mistake, then walking into a pit of success will be like trying to cross a minefield, where every move can have serious consequences. In this type of emotional battlefield, you are validated or invalidated by every choice, action, and outcome. You face an exhausting life, where avoidance of risk feels like the only logical choice.

Fortunately, researchers have found that you can get out of this minefield mentality by focusing on discovery. No longer are unwanted outcomes your judge and jury; they are now your teacher.

When you focus on discovery, you have more control over each moment, and you accept that you must take steps and practice to achieve your desired outcome. You do not expect to always be good the first or second or even third time. You only expect to discover ways to become better. You shift the internal dialogue from "What if I fail?" to "What can I learn or discover from each step?" A discovery focus could include these questions:

- What skill will help me get to the goal?
- What can I learn from the problems that just occurred?
- What can I learn from each attempt?
- What can I do differently next time?
- What building block do I need next?

The answers to these questions make no judgments about your value or abilities. They simply describe the situation so that you can improve the next step. Thus, the pit becomes a big laboratory of discovering what works and what does not, rather than a test of your value.

An additional benefit of focusing on discovery is that when you learn something new that you care about, your brain sends out dopamine and serotonin, creating a sense of euphoria, satisfaction, and confidence that motivates you to keep moving toward your goal. You experience that joy of "Wow! I just figured that out!" The more often this set of chemicals flows, the more you see yourself as capable and the more motivated you are to move forward.

And to be clear, focusing on discovery does not mean that you ignore the end goal. You are not becoming that sports parent who tells the kids that a loss does not matter as long as they had fun. Of course, winning and accomplishing a task is fun. However, focusing on discovery creates more wins along the way and gives you momentum to achieve your end goal.

When you add a discovery focus to embracing the pit, you will tend to say things like these when you encounter difficulties:

- I did not get this the first time. I wonder what I need to learn or practice.
- Yes, that choice did not work. I messed up. What should I try next?
- I have not done this before. It will take more time than normal.
- Who can I call for advice, feedback, or other help?
- I do not have this yet. Tough things are worth the effort.

The judgments about your detours, mistakes, and misfortunes are reduced with this approach, and the confidence to take the next step is increased. As you learn to discover, you become more of an observer of what happened than a critic. Remember, you are not supposed to know how to navigate your current pit yet. You have never done it before.

No one has ever achieved something of value without doing it poorly at first (e.g., learning a language, leading a meeting, developing a new skill). Although you can never know how many steps your next goal will take, you can make each step count. Every step increases your level of experience when you focus on discovery. When you make a new discovery, even a small one, it is a time to celebrate.

Narrow Your Scope

Sometimes you may think that, to succeed, you have to do every-thing now and do it all really well. But you are not trying to leap across a pit; you are learning to navigate it. When it comes to embracing the pit and moving more quickly through it, less really is more. Organizational researchers Chris McChesney, Sean Covey, and Jim Huling have shown that the fewer goals your organization intentionally focuses on, the more likely your group is to achieve those goals. Conversely, organizations with many goals are less likely to achieve any of them. At an individual level, this means that rather than attempting to learn five skills at once, narrowing your scope to focus on one or two skills (and the building blocks of those skills) will accelerate your learning and reduce your burden.

For example, of the many studies that demonstrate the power of narrowing your focus, one of our favorites highlights the differences between professional and amateur musicians. When learning a song, amateur musicians will play through the whole song over and over, anchoring bad habits. Then, after a few minutes of limited progress, they spontaneously start playing a song they already know and spend the rest of their practice time on familiar tunes. This method is an inefficient, frustrating way to learn music.

In contrast, professional musicians narrow their focus to master a new song quickly. The professional takes a segment of a song and works it until proficiency is achieved. Then, the musician selects a new section, and the process repeats. Little of the precious practice time is spent on what the professional already knows or in playing the whole song through. Thus, professional musicians achieve mastery faster because they focus on the building block they need most.

This same approach of narrowing your focus applies to learning any other skill. For example, if you are a manager, a parent, or a friend wanting to improve your communication skills, rather than trying to get good at multiple skills all at once, you are better off focusing on first developing your listening skills. Once you achieve proficiency, you can then focus on a new skill. Remember, your brain learns with focus and repetition.

Seek Advice and Feedback

Many people avoid asking for advice for fear of looking incompetent. A study by researchers from Harvard University and the Wharton School of the University of Pennsylvania, however, found that people who asked for advice on difficult issues were rated as more competent than were those who did not seek input. Furthermore, people who asked for advice also felt better about themselves than did those who did not ask. Seeking advice makes it easier to navigate the pit of success.

By obtaining advice, you avoid unnecessary detours, minimize mistakes, and identify essential skills. Getting advice or feedback can be as easy as seeking out a colleague, connecting with a current or former manager, or finding a subject-matter expert for guidance. In some cases, hiring a professional is the best way to embrace the pit. These different experts can give essential guidance and feedback on your performance to help you succeed faster and with less confusion. Learning to receive feedback rather than defend your actions is the fast pass to learning.

You do not have to embrace your pit of success by yourself. Asking for advice and feedback gives you knowledge, guidance, and support to make the journey much easier. Most people are willing to help a person who asks for advice; they just need an invitation. You are not alone.

Embracing Your Future

Whether you chose a pit, like Brandon's new consulting job, or had a pit imposed on you, feeling overwhelmed is normal, and people at all levels experience confusion and doubts. The lack of context, the need for new skills, time pressures, and unknowns can create a deep pit. No matter the type of pit, you will be asked to do hard things that lie beyond your experience.

When you embrace your pit of success, you will reduce the burden of your journey and learn faster. Both chosen and imposed pits can be your ally.

Key Ideas

- Both chosen and imposed pits of success require you to do hard things beyond your level of experience.
- Avoidance is natural. You want to protect yourself from potential mistakes, pain, embarrassment, doubt, loss, unneeded effort, and feelings of inadequacy; you are not stupid! The problem, however, is not your desire to protect yourself from pain. The challenge is knowing when to stop protecting yourself from these difficulties.
- Embracing your pit of success is about pragmatism, not optimism: you do not have to love, want, or need what has happened to you.
- Five approaches that make embracing the pit easier:
  - Find a why (a purpose).
  - Redefine your state of betweenness as something beneficial.
  - Focus on discovery while pursuing the end result.
  - Narrow your scope to achieve more.
  - Ask for advice and feedback.
- Clarifying the organizational why or purpose can make it easier for individuals to find their own why.
- When you embrace a pit—chosen or imposed—you reduce the burden of your journey.

Frequently Asked Questions About Embracing the Pit

Shouldn't I just focus on my strengths? Strengths are a great place to start from. If your strengths will solve the problems in your path, then you should absolutely use your strengths. If, however, the demands have changed and your current strengths are not working, then it is probably time to embrace a pit of success and use the new demands to their best advantage. You are unlikely to succeed over a long period by only focusing on your current strengths in a changing environment. Focusing on purpose and the bigger challenges to be solved will guide you on whether to stick with a strength or embrace a pit of success and develop a new strength.

How long should I stay in the pit? That answer is made on a case-by-case basis. If you are doing a job in a new industry, you may not feel truly comfortable for several months or even a few years. Your previous experience and your purpose, goals, and support affect how long you will remain in the pit. I know one lawyer who changed her area of expertise, and it took her four years before she felt like an expert again. It is not uncommon to take a year or more to feel comfortable in a new pit.

Should I embrace every pit? Absolutely not. Some pits are not right for you, or the timing is not right. Learning to ride a motorcycle, seeking a promotion, learning to play the piano, or moving to a new country may not be right for you right now (or ever). Developing clarity about your purpose helps you make these decisions.

Some pits are unavoidable. You have no choice about being there; you are stuck in that pit. But when you embrace its challenges, you can reduce your suffering from this unwanted demand.

Is there some way I can just avoid a pit completely? In a stable and predictable environment, you can rely on your present and past skills and avoid the pit. In a changing world, however, learning depends on your doing things that make you feel temporarily incompetent. Ask yourself if this pit aligns with your purpose. You do not have to simultaneously be the PTA president, the volunteer soccer coach, and the top performer at work, while also having the best yard and competing in a triathlon. Intentionally reducing the number of pits gives you more capacity for ones that matter most.

Will I always be in a pit? While it sometimes feels as though life is just one continuous pit after another, if you always find yourself in unwanted pits, you may want to look at which decisions, skills, and relationships you can influence. You always have the power to change your situation in some small way. The principles in this chapter and later chapters will help you take more control and make facing your pits easier.

Is there a way to get through the pit faster? Everyone's speed is different. Your learning curve will be based on your experience, genetics, and motivation. To speed up your learning, you can redefine the hard things, clarify your purpose, find the building block you need, and develop the required skills. Reducing the current number of demands and asking for help can also accelerate your learning.

But what if I fail one more time? Yes, you might fail. Failure is not necessarily a bad thing. It is a step in the learning process. No fails—no steps forward. Why should you and I be excused from the privilege of failing and then figuring out a better way? Few things of value can be achieved the first time. The goal is to learn a little more from each experience, not to master a skill in a single leap. With the right practice and building blocks, your brain can and will make the connections it needs for success.

Is it OK to stay where I am for a while? Yes, absolutely! You do not need to be racing into another pit all the time. Sometimes you can use a breather. There are times to really enjoy your expertise, but there are times when you need to let go of your expertise and embrace the unknown. The wisdom to know the difference is the challenge everyone faces.

What if I embrace a pit and decide I do not want to keep going? Usually, that is fine. You cannot always know until you try. Only 27 percent of college graduates are working in a job related to their major. Life does not provide a crystal ball to tell you exactly what you will get out of every experience before you have it. Some pits need to be abandoned in favor of a different approach. Other pits, however, require much more effort and practice before a goal is reached. For these pits, you do not want to quit too soon. Your clarity of purpose can help you decide whether to stick with your choice or drop it.

How long do I have to feel like an idiot? When you start focusing on discovery and developing building blocks, the fear of feeling stupid is reduced or eliminated. You have permission to *not* know and to be confused. Not knowing something or taking longer to learn a skill does not make you an idiot. The doubts are not a sign of incompetence but are rather an indication that you are in a place where you can learn.

CHAPTER 4

Trade Up

Audra McDonald is a six-time Tony Award–winning Broadway legend, an American Theatre Hall of Fame member, and a recipient of *Time* magazine's Top 100 Most Influential People Award. Her beautiful voice and engaging presence captivate audiences around the world in such performances as *Beauty and the Beast*, *Ragtime*, and *Porgy and Bess*. One performance, however, did not go as planned.

Audra was selected as a featured singer at an award ceremony whose venue was different from her Broadway home. As she walked onstage and looked out into the audience, a giant screen in back forced her to see herself. It was like a massive mirror magnifying everything about her.

Notwithstanding her experience performing for hundreds of large audiences in many diverse locations, this stage was different. She became distracted at seeing herself on the big screen—her face, her mouth, her hair, and her expressions all diverted her attention. She lost focus and began an internal dialogue as she was singing.

"Is that what I look like?" she asked herself. "I can't believe I make that face. I shouldn't do that. My hair is out of place."

Audra became so focused on the image on the screen that she forgot the words to the song. She stopped her performance, tried to lighten the tension with a few humorous words, and then started over. Despite her broad experience, this new venue was a pit that caused Audra to focus on the wrong thing at the wrong time.

Companies can make the same mistake. IKEA focused on the wrong thing at the wrong time when it first entered the U.S. market in the 1980s. The executives where trying to force the U.S. consumer to adopt metric-sized beds, but they were not making much progress. Given the success of these beds in other countries, the leaders in the Netherlands held tight to the belief that customers in the United States should adjust their purchasing habits. However, the consumers would not change their home preferences to fit these metric beds.

IKEA offered specials to customers and incentives to its salespeople, but the mattresses continued to stack up in the warehouse. The U.S. management implored the executives to shift their strategy, but the corporate leaders kept insisting that these metric beds should sell as well as they had in other countries. The executives were focused on what had worked in the past (the wrong thing) and ignored the current environment (the wrong time), where American king, queen, and twin sizing ruled.

Channelized Attention

Losing awareness and becoming hyperfocused on the wrong thing is a phenomenon known as *channelized attention*. This phenomenon was first studied in World War II, when fighter pilots would focus so intently on their target that they would lose situational awareness and smash into their target with their plane. The same phenomenon happens on the freeway when drivers are staring at the back of the truck in front of them and end up driving right into it or when people are texting in the car at a red light and end up sitting at the light after it has turned green.

Everyone is susceptible to channelized attention; we can all get hooked and focus on the wrong thing at the wrong time. At work, the phenomenon shows up when you focus on maintaining an out-of-date process rather than taking the time to fix it. Or you constantly question whether you are good enough to learn a new skill. Or you find yourself reading your email in meetings and believing that you can pay attention to the presenter at the same time. When your attention is channelized, you jeopardize better results, positive relationships, and safety.

In this chapter, we will discuss ways you unintentionally channelize your focus and limit your ability to navigate the pit. In the next chapter, we will look at ways to focus on the right things at the right time so that you can trade up and become more adaptive.

Is Your Focus Limiting You?

In our research, we have found that leaders can easily get channelized on different issues, but there are five limiting types of focus that leaders routinely get hooked on:

- *Focusing on "stuck"*: There is nothing I can do to change the situation.
- *Focusing on "should"*: The world should be different than it is.
- *Focusing on "fear"*: I am not good enough in so many ways.
- *Focusing on "hurt"*: I am always going to be minimized and ignored.
- *Focusing on "justified"*: I have a right to behave this way. It is their fault. The end justifies the means.

While these five limiters are not the only ways to focus on the wrong thing at the wrong time, they often lie at the root of someone's inability to navigate a pit of success. And unfortunately, the more you focus on these limiters, the more likely you will become channelized and unable to build a path forward.

If you focus on any of these five limiters, it does not mean that you are a bad person or lack control. An initial focus is a normal and logical way to protect yourself and to draw attention to real problems. As you read the descriptions of these limiters, distinguish between the times you may need to temporarily visit them and those times when you may overfocus on them and get channelized.

Focusing on "Stuck"

When you focus on being *stuck*, you believe that the pit of success you are facing is bigger than you. You feel unable to influence the challenges you must face. Feeling stuck can be a result of multiple failed attempts, not knowing the steps forward, lacking resources, or doubting your ability to learn.

A *stuck* focus creates a belief that you can never get out from under the weight you carry and can never solve the problems you must face. In this state, you see yourself as inadequate, the burdens as unending, and your efforts futile. Essentially, you believe your brain cannot be changed.

Phrases you may rely on include these:

- This always happens to me.
- I'm never good at this.
- I'll never figure this out. I'm not good enough.
- Why bother? Why try? It won't matter.
- Yeah, but …

If you get overly focused on being *stuck*, you can always find reasons to avoid taking action or to keep doing what you have always done. After all, if you are truly stuck, any effort is a waste of time. Thus, quitting, feeling defeated, or blaming can feel logical and even inevitable.

Focusing on "Should"

When you impose strong demands on the world—or yourself—about how things must be, you tend to see the world in black-and-white terms. You look at how everything *should* be, not the way it is. You believe that this pit of success should be different, that the world and others should respond in another way, and that you should be more intelligent or capable. With this focus on the *should* instead of the *is*, you demand a kinder, fairer, or more predictable experience. And if you are deeply channelized on *should*, your desires become a demand—an imperative—of how things must be. Otherwise, you feel cheated that life is not meeting your expectations.

With this focus, you think that events should always work out as planned and that results should be guaranteed. Because you believe your criteria seem logical, when things do not work out as expected, you may feel betrayed, ignored, or hurt by management, friends, family, or God.

Here are some typical phrases that might emerge when you are focused on *should*:

- But I planned it all out. I did my part. I deserve to have this.
- I (*or* they) shouldn't make mistakes.
- I (*or* they) should be doing more.
- I should have been included.
- Customers should keep doing this.

As you encounter negative situations, you may even feel anger toward yourself or others about how things should be. *Should* is an easy and natural place to focus on when things are beyond your ability to control. But the more you focus on what should be, the less you focus on what is and what you can do about it.

Focusing on "Fear"

When you focus on *fear*, you worry deeply that you are not good enough—physically, emotionally, socially, intellectually, financially, or spiritually. You believe that what it takes to achieve success, master a skill, or gain safety, acceptance, or love lies outside your reach. At some level, you see the potential for personal failure in whatever you embrace. Any mistakes or missteps become a heavy burden because they confirm an existing fear of inadequacy or great risk.

You might declare statements like these if you are focusing on *fear*:

- Maybe I'm just not good enough.
- I feel at risk.
- I'll probably fail.
- What if my actions mess up others?
- I'm probably just not capable (*or* lovable, special, etc.).

Of course, some level of fear can help you avoid danger and prompt beneficial action. But when you focus on fear excessively, you lose your ability to make productive choices, take appropriate risks, and move forward. A *fear* focus paralyzes you and separates you from what you want most.

Focusing on "Hurt"

With disappointments, slights, and injustices happening to everyone, *hurt* is a normal part of life. But when you are in the pit of success, these pains can magnify, causing you to become channelized and feel offended, sad, left out, and betrayed more often and for longer periods. This unresolved hurt can create anger toward others or yourself. Of course, bad things do happen and can deserve some anger. But when you become overly fixed on these wounding events, the pain dominates your thinking and limits your ability to manage the demands of the pit.

Here are a few ways you might explain the world when you focus on *hurt*:

- Why do people keep doing this to me?
- Why is the world against me?
- I should have known better than to think they would care.
- I'm so mad that I'm not wanted here.
- Why do they keep ignoring me?

Sometimes, noticing *hurt* can be helpful because it leads to healthy action such as avoiding toxic relationships or changing your approach. But when these feelings feed on themselves, you begin a downward spiral that adds suffering to your already-negative situation.

Focusing on "Justified"

When you focus on *justified*, you seek to adjust the scales of life because what seems rightfully yours (or others') has been unfairly taken away. Because the scales are out of balance, you think you have a right to blame, demand, hold grudges, and be the equalizer that restores order. At these moments, you believe that the end justifies the means and that you are above the rules. Because the world has set the terms of the conflict, you feel justified in behaving any way you see fit to address the problem.

Typical phrases you might use when you focus on *justified* include these:

- They set the terms of the fight; I'm just responding.
- It's really their fault. They are to blame.
- No one talks to me that way. I will show them.
- I deserve *my* share.
- I have a *right* to do this. They started this conflict.

Although some of these statements may indeed contain elements of truth, this state of perceived superiority nevertheless limits your ability to see the bigger picture.

Recognizing Channelized Thinking

Everyone sometimes focuses on one or more of these limiting thoughts. They are the realities that occur when you are pushed beyond your experience and start concentrating on the wrong thing at the wrong time. However, no one must stay channelized on a thought that is not working. As you become aware of a limiting focus, you can reduce its negative impact on you, others, and your business.

As a starting point, ask yourself these questions:

- When, if at all, do I focus on a limiter (*stuck, should, hurt, fear, justified*, or another limiting focus)?
- What are my mental, verbal, and physical responses when I focus on any of these limiters?

- What are the advantages (e.g., protection, avoidance of risk) and the disadvantages (e.g., reduced effort, fewer options) of the focus?
- Is my department or business overly focused on the wrong thing at the wrong time?

Letting Go of Channelized Attention

When you are in your pit of success, there are so many unknowns and pressures that it is easy to get lost and focus on the wrong things. The IKEA executives succumbed to two types of channelized thinking. First, they thought that the U.S. market should adopt their product, and, second, they felt justified by their past success. The executives definitely spent too much time focusing on what customers should buy instead of what they would buy. Once the leaders switched their focus, their profits increased.

As we described at the beginning of this chapter, Audra McDonald felt quite embarrassed about her performance. She had focused on the wrong thing at the wrong time, yet she quickly switched her focus in the moment and was able to complete the song. She did not let that moment define her; she resisted focusing on being *hurt, afraid, or stuck*. She instead learned that she needed to find a better focus when jumbo screens mirrored her every move. Audra turned her painful experience into a teachable moment, not a judgmental one. She traded up.

Key Ideas

- You channelize your attention when you focus on something so intently that you become less aware of the broader context. You are focusing on the wrong thing at the wrong time.

- Everyone experiences some type of channelized attention, but left unchecked, it can limit your success.

- Five primary types of focus that limit you are *stuck*, *should*, *hurt*, *fear*, and *justified*.

- Just as individuals can become channelized, a business—a collective of individuals—can be channelized on one or more of these limiting focuses. A business can trade up its focus as leaders focus on the right things at the right time.

CHAPTER 5

Trade Up (and Up)

Seventeen-year-old Steven Ortiz of Glendora, California, got serious about trading up. Using Craigslist, he traded a cell phone for an iPad Touch, and then traded the iPad for a motorcycle. This process of trading continued over two years, and after fourteen trades, he owned a fully running Porsche Boxster worth several thousand dollars. This outcome was not the result of an accidental or lucky trade. Steven was intentional about trading up for something better than he had.

You too can trade up and up. But rather than a cell phone for a Porsche, you can trade a limiting focus for an adaptive focus. To trade up, you start with what you have and then find something a little bit better until you get what you want. Whether you have a difficult assignment, an uncooperative team member, a life trauma, a betrayal, or self-doubt, you can trade up your focus and increase the ease of achieving your goal.

A few years ago, Jacob (not his real name), the founder and leader of a professional music group, came to one of us (Dave) for help in performing live. He had just released a new album, and his producer wanted him to do more live performances to promote the album. Jacob, however, was struggling with extreme nervousness in live performances. He enjoyed creating music in the studio, but as happens with many performers, his anxiety increased when he looked out at the audience.

His challenge was that he focused on getting the audience's approval and feared the judgment of the crowd. He was focusing on the wrong thing at the wrong time. To make a change, he first had to become aware of his focus and then find a more beneficial one. By gradually refocusing on the things he wanted to give to the audience—his great message and beautiful music—he learned to successfully perform with confidence. He and his enthusiastic fans benefited when he traded up from *taking from* the audience to *giving to* the audience.

Likewise, when you encounter a pit of success (e.g., speaking up in a meeting, influencing executives, interviewing for a job, starting a new position, getting feedback, learning to parent), there are ways to trade up your focus. It is what your brain is designed to do.

Your Brain Can Change Focus

While your brain is estimated to have over twenty-one hundred thoughts per hour, you can selectively focus on which thoughts receive the most attention. For example, if you are at a noisy party with a hundred people talking, music blaring, and glasses clinking, you can choose to listen to the person next to you, the conversation behind you, or the music. You hear and magnify what you pay attention to.

Robert Wiseman, professor of psychology at the University of Hertfordshire in England, demonstrated that people could be

trained to selectively focus their attention and actions to become "luckier." With only thirty days of training and practice, 80 percent of the unlucky people in the study became significantly luckier in this short time, reporting increases in job promotions, fewer accidents, and new relationships. Being unlucky was not a fixed trait that these people were born with but, rather, a focus they could switch to change their luck at work, home, and social settings.

This ability to refocus affects business leaders in similar ways. Jeffrey Dyer, the best-selling author of *The Innovator's DNA*, analyzed the difference between the most innovative CEOs (Steve Jobs, Jeff Bezos, etc.) and the more "delivery-focused" leaders. He found that the innovative CEOs spent more time in innovative behaviors (associating, questioning, observing, networking, and experimenting). They thought more about innovation and allowed more time for it in the organization than did the other CEOs. In follow-up research, Dyer and his colleagues found that although some leaders defined themselves as noninnovative, they could be trained to switch their focus to behaviors that increased their own and their teams' innovation.

You too can choose which stimulus—thought, words, or behavior—gets more of your attention. Your brain can switch at your command and you can trade up your results.

Three Paths to Trading Up

Remember, you do not have to trade your focus up to a Porsche level in a single step. You simply need to start where you are and begin looking in the right direction. As you become more intentional in your focus, you can improve your results.

You can trade up your focus in three primary ways: you can interrupt it, name it, or replace it. Any one of these approaches could help you break the cycle of focusing on the wrong thing at the wrong time and make it easier to navigate your pit of success. It does not matter which trade you start with; the key is to make a trade for something better than what you currently have. Consider how you may use each of these pathways to trading up.

Interrupt It

Interruption is a powerful tool to help you break the cycle of limiter thoughts and become more adaptive. Across disciplines, the power of interruption has been shown to improve innovation, safety, and health and to reduce depression and interpersonal conflict. Consider the impact of an interruption when couples are arguing.

The "Wait for the Equipment" Interruption

Disagreements between couples can sometimes become quite heated. Emotions can rise quickly, and logic can fall to an all-time low. These interactions can make two people who care about each other behave in ways that damage the relationship. To improve these interactions, John Gottman, a renowned marriage researcher, developed a study to investigate whether the trajectory of these downward-spiraling encounters could be changed by a simple interruption.

In the study, Gottman asked couples to come into a lab where their conversations would be videotaped for research purposes. Each couple was then asked to discuss a topic that they disagreed on. As they talked, the interactions became more antagonistic, and personal attacks often replaced calm discussion. Fifteen minutes into each discussion, one of the researchers would enter the room and ask the couple to pause their discussion, informing them that there had been a video equipment malfunction. During this time, the couple was asked to refrain from talking with each other. After thirty minutes of waiting, the couple was told that the equipment had been fixed and that they should continue their discussion.

Researchers found that after this manufactured interruption, the tone between each couple changed. Instead of a heated interchange with sharp words and accusations, they began talking to each other with more respect. Even their heart rates had slowed to a normal rate. The simple interruption of pausing the argument to wait for the equipment had allowed their brains to quit focusing on the wrong thing at the wrong time.

When you interrupt a limiting focus, you break the cycle of channelized attention and give space for a more adaptive response. Your brain may only need a moment to pull out of its current cycle to consider a different path forward.

More Ways to Interrupt Your Focus
You have many options to interrupt your focus. No single interruption will work all the time, but choosing a go-to interruption is helpful. Over time, you can adopt different interruptions if the initial one does not work.

Here are just a few options you could consider:

- *Plan a delay:* Take a break, plan on dealing with the issue in five minutes or tomorrow, listen to good music, play the piano, or start a timer.
- *Change locations:* Walk outside, go into the garden, move to another room, or sit in a different chair.
- *Ask yourself a question:* "What problem am I trying to solve?" "What do I need?" "What am I concerned about losing?"
- *Adopt a phrase:* "I will work on this later." "Not now." "This too shall pass." Find a phrase that works for you.
- *Breathe:* Yes, you have heard this advice a thousand times before. There is a reason that it is so common. Breathing really works. Deep breaths activate your parasympathetic nervous system, telling your body and brain to calm down. Breathing away the tension or a limiting thought can truly work, and it works best if you have practiced.
- *Create a prewritten interruption card:* Write out a plan on a card. It may say, "I know this is temporary," "I can deal with this in ten minutes," "Time for a walk," or "I'm OK. I'll figure this out with a little time." Write a favorite quote on it. Write instructions on how to breathe. The act of reading the card interrupts the downward cycle.
- *Start writing your thoughts:* Using a blank sheet of paper or journal, write down your thoughts, hopes, fears, and other emotions. Draw a picture. Write a story.

Interruptions help you break the cycle of focusing on the wrong thing at the wrong time. They open the door to trading up.

Name It

You can reduce the impact of a limiting focus by giving it a name. When you name what you are feeling, experiencing, or focusing on, your brain literally takes more control over your situation so that you can trade up.

Moving Thoughts in Your Brain

A team of researchers at the University of California, Los Angeles, used fMRI to demonstrate that the brain changes as people put words to their experiences. To study this effect, the researchers evaluated brain activity in volunteers as they viewed pictures with emotionally charged faces (happy, angry, surprised, etc.). The fMRI showed that the amygdala lit up as the study participants reviewed pictures showing intensely negative emotions. (The amygdala is the part of the brain that processes emotions, telling your body to fight, flee, or freeze.)

When the participants named the emotions, however, the location of brain activity shifted to the prefrontal cortex (also known as the executive brain). Instead of the amygdala lighting up with fight, flight, or freeze responses, the prefrontal cortex, responsible for complex problem-solving and decision-making, became active. Thus, when you verbally describe an issue or a feeling, you increase your ability to solve the problem in front of you. Matthew Lieberman, professor of psychiatry and biobehavioral sciences and the lead researcher of the UCLA experiment, summarized the team's findings: "Assessing and naming the emotion seems to transform the emotion into an object of scrutiny thereby disrupting its raw intensity."

Naming what you are experiencing orients you to where you are and puts you in charge of where you want to go. Or as author and psychiatrist Daniel Siegel says, "Name it to Tame it."

Think It, Say It, or Write It

To overcome the focus that is hijacking your current emotions and behaviors, simply ask yourself, "What am I experiencing or feeling?" Just answering the question gets your brain working in your favor.

When you answer the question, you may prefer to think the answer, verbalize it, or write it down. The format does not matter; each approach helps you trade up from having your amygdala in charge to giving your prefrontal cortex the driver's seat.

Consider these examples that put your executive brain in charge:

- You get shot down or ignored in a meeting. → "I feel hurt and powerless."
- You get asked to do something beyond your experience → "I feel afraid I will fail."
- People are not doing what needs to be done → "I feel powerless, ripped off, and stuck."

You are not predestined to be stuck focusing on the wrong thing at the wrong time. As you name it, you will start trading up.

Replace It

Your brain is really bad at focusing on more than one thing at once. But that limitation works to your advantage: as your brain gets a signal to focus on something new, it spends less of its resources on the previous focus. As new neural pathways are being ignited, by default the old pathways are being fired less. You are deprioritizing the limiting thought and prioritizing the new thought.

Consider the case of one executive who needed to trade up and replace his limiting focus.

Finding a Better Focus

One executive who was totally hooked on *should* came to me (Amy) looking for a way to improve his leadership. Weighed down by multiple decisions, he thought he should adjust his choices to the needs of the twenty-five people in his organization and should accommodate the competing priorities of other executives. As a result, the team members were frequently confused by contradictory priorities, unmade decisions, and changing goals.

As I helped him become aware that his *should* list was limiting rather than benefiting his business, he began focusing on the purpose that was driving him and the business. This changed outlook enabled him to focus more on the direction he truly wanted to pursue, rather than on what he thought he should be doing. Adjusting his focus allowed him to choose higher-priority issues, make decisions with more confidence, and get the team aligned on goals that lasted. His life of *should* was traded up to a focus on purpose and direction.

Trades You Can Make

While you can focus on many worthwhile issues to replace a limiting focus, having a few go-to trades can accelerate the trade-up process. The following chart provides seven questions that can move you from a limiting focus to an adaptive focus.

These trades give you more of what you want. The intent is not that you would ask all the questions in any moment or that all

Limiting Focus → Adaptive Focus

Limiting Focus	Adaptive Focus
Stuck	What is happening?
Should	What is my purpose or direction?
Fear	What can I learn or discover?
Hurt	What can I control or influence?
Justified	What if I could ___? What if I had ___?
	What am I grateful for?
	What small action can I take?

questions apply in every situation. You may find that one question is enough to move you away from a limiting focus, or you may need multiple questions to trade up. The key is to start practicing a few questions until they become habit.

- *What is happening (or has happened)?* Describe accurately—without judgment or catastrophizing—what is happening at this moment or what has already occurred. Decide to focus on what is, not what should have been.

- *What is my purpose or direction?* Purpose gives you a reason to persist. It answers the question *why?*

- *What do I want to learn or discover?* When you focus on discovery, your circumstances become your teacher rather than your judge.

- *What can I control or influence?* While many things may be out of your control, focusing on those things will keep you stuck. Focusing on what you can control gives you a path forward.

- *What if?* The power of considering "what if?" enables you to create new options. As you ask what-if questions, your mind can look at the problem in new ways. You always have more options than you think (see the next chapter).

- *What am I grateful for?* A sense of gratitude does not diminish or ignore the realities of the challenges you are facing, but gratitude assesses what you do have and establishes that perhaps not everything is a complete disaster. Acknowledging that you have something puts you in a mindset of abundance rather than one of scarcity. It is easier to move forward when you understand that you already have something.

- *What is the smallest action I can take?* While you may not be able to overcome a big obstacle immediately, there is always something you can act on. Once you start moving, it is easier to keep moving forward. Small steps are sustainable, and when you act on them, you can solve bigger issues.

Remember, you do not need a perfect focus to trade up; the goal is to adopt a focus that is better than your current limiting focus. Use the adaptive focus questions discussed here, and add your own favorite trades to get more of what you want. Whatever challenge you are facing, you can switch your focus and better navigate your pit of success.

And while we know that you can always trade up, we want to add one word of caution to this helpful tool: not every trade is appropriate for every situation. For example, to trade up to gratitude for abuse is not healthy. To say you should embrace toxic or abusive situations makes no sense. But deciding to take action to increase your physical and mental safety does. The question to ask in these difficult circumstances is, "How can I trade up in *healthy* ways?"

Trade Up for a Better Life

To illustrate the lifelong implications of trading up and replacing a limiting focus, I (Dave) will close this chapter with a personal story from my daughter's life (with her permission). This story has inspired me on just how much you can trade up.

When my daughter was twelve, she loved dancing and was active in competitions and dance performances. During this time, however, she began to complain more and more that her feet were hurting. My wife and I spent the next two years taking her to different doctors, trying to figure out why she was in so much pain. No one had answers.

The pain grew until finally it was so severe that she had to start using a wheelchair. She dropped out of school and began to home school so that she could study on the days she was not in excruciating pain. Just as bad as the physical pain was the emotional pain she also endured because she was separated from her friends and classmates. They did not know how to play and interact with someone in constant pain and in a wheelchair.

Despite working with a neurologist and undergoing multiple all-day hospital treatments and various medication experiments, my daughter still had no clear answers, and by the time she was fifteen, she was becoming more depressed. My daughter's identity started to become intertwined with her daily chronic pain. The prospect of being in continuous pain and needing to use a wheelchair for the rest of her life descended on her like a dark, impenetrable cloud.

One day, as she sat alone in her room thinking of her future in a wheelchair—in pain, without dance, and without friends—she had a thought: "I can be miserable my whole life, or I can move on. I choose to move on." She still had incredible pain, could not predict if she would be stuck in bed on any given day, and still needed a wheelchair, but she decided to focus on what she could control.

She did not have a naive view that everything was fine and would magically get better. Instead, it was a pragmatic view to move away from a focus on *stuck*, *should*, and the unfairness of her situation and to instead accept the reality she had been given. Fortunately, after several years of various treatments, she now walks most days, and the pain is mostly manageable.

This medical success and my daughter's ability to walk again may seem like the happy ending to a tragic story, but these achievements were not the real victory. The real success was her decision to face her illness and her life by trading up her focus. Her choice was not based on whether she would walk or be out of pain. Instead, she decided how she would face life *with* the pain. In some ways, that choice changed her life even more than did the ability to walk again. By replacing her focus, she became free. She navigated a pit of success from a very depressing and lonely place. She traded up.

You do not need to live channelized in the worlds of *stuck*, *should*, *hurt*, *fear*, *justified*, or any other limiting focus. You can train yourself to trade up and focus on things that help you navigate your pit of success. Even a small trade can make a huge difference in your confidence, peace of mind, and other aspects of your life or business. No matter where you are, you can always trade up.

Key Ideas

- Your brain can selectively attend to what you direct it to pay attention to. Not only does switching your focus increase your luck, but you can also increase your ability to perform under pressure, innovate, and find new solutions.
- Three ways to trade up your focus are to interrupt the focus, to name it, and to replace it.
- When you name an emotion, you move it from the amygdala (emotion-processing part of the brain) to the prefrontal cortex (decision-making part of the brain).
- To trade up your focus and become more adaptive, ask any of these questions:
  - What *is* happening?
  - What is my purpose or direction?
  - What can I learn or discover?
  - What can I control or influence?
  - What if I could ___? What if I had ___?
  - What am I grateful for?
  - What small action can I take?
- You can achieve more of what you want when you trade up your focus.

CHAPTER 6

Make Something from Nothing

"Houston, we've had a problem" is one of the most famous phrases of the last fifty years.* These alarming words were uttered by pilot John Swigert fifty-five hours into the Apollo 13 flight to the moon. The explosion of an oxygen tank in the service module had created a series of events that caused the cabin to fill with carbon monoxide. All three astronauts aboard would die if they could not fix an air filter in the lunar module, which would have to serve as their rescue craft for returning to earth. But to fix the filter, they literally had to make a 9-by-9-inch filter fit into a 15-inch long cylinder with a diameter of 5 inches.

If they tried to cut the filter down to force it into the hole, the filter would have been destroyed and been unusable; they had to keep the 9-inch-square filter intact. The National Aeronautics and Space Administration (NASA) support team at the Mission Control in Houston had to figure out how to make the mismatched filter system work while the disaster clock kept ticking.

---

* Note: In the movie "Apollo 13," Tom Hanks states, "Houston, we have a problem."

In approaching the task, the NASA team could have become hung up on the fact that a 9-inch-square box would not fit into a 5-inch-diameter hole. They could have questioned why they had not stowed an extra 5-inch filter aboard the spacecraft before it left earth. Or they could have regretted that they did not train for this contingency. They could also have focused on how these parts had never been designed to be used this way. Or they could have complained about what they did not have. And most dreadful of all, they could have focused on what they would say to the families of the astronauts who would not return.

Instead, the team members focused on finding optimal ways to use what they had. The team in Houston gathered all the objects that were available to the astronauts and started looking at new ways to use these resources. They decided that what they needed to solve the problem was within their reach.

The result was an unlikely combination of objects:

- Two 9-inch-square filters
- A pair of socks
- The cardboard cover of a flight manual
- Two hoses pulled from a space suit
- Two plastic bags
- A bungee cord
- Duct tape

The astronauts placed each 9-inch filter inside a plastic bag, which they tore to insert the hose. They put the manual cover in the bag to provide strength so that the hose would not be crushed as it was installed. The socks were inserted into a ventilation hole in the filter to keep carbon-monoxide-filled air from bypassing the filter. The astronauts used duct tape to prevent air leakage and to hold things in place. They attached the hoses to the ventilation intake on the lunar module. Finally, they used a bungee cord to hold the device in place against the wall. This unsophisticated filter assemblage brought three astronauts home to their families.

A pit of success can force seemingly impossible challenges on you, situations where you do not have all the answers, supplies, support, influence, tools, experience, time, and other support that you wish you had. While your situation may not be as life-threatening as it was for Apollo 13, your demands can make you feel inadequate, frustrated, and out of options. But you too can discover that what you need lies within your reach. You can make something out of nothing and create real solutions.

Your Brain Without Options

Your brain loves autonomy, and the perception of autonomy is a place of comfort and power. A primary path to a sense of autonomy is having options or believing that you have them. Unfortunately, when you are in a pit of success and believe you have no options, your brain focuses on feeling stuck.

In this condition, your brain floods your system with a variety of self-inhibiting chemicals because it believes it is under threat. According to Steven Maier and Linda Watkins, neuroscience researchers from the University of Colorado, Boulder, one of the chief culprits is a serotonin imbalance, which can create a sense of helplessness. This and other chemicals create debilitating activity in your amygdala (emotion center of your brain), hippocampus (memory center of your brain), and medial prefrontal cortex (decision-making center of your brain).

Your response might be passivity or aggression. In both conditions, however, you are no longer focused on solving the problem. Instead, you inadvertently develop a limiting focus that makes you feel even more helpless and stuck.

One catalyst for this cycle is your perceived explanation of why the situation exists. How you define your situation affects how the brain deals with the problem. Three of the most common explanations that start the downward cycle of feeling stuck are these: "I'm incapable," "The problem is unsolvable," and "The environment is unchangeable." This triple threat gives you every reason to quit.

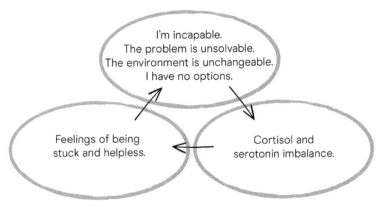

- *I'm incapable:* You assume that you lack the skills, intelligence, strength, relationships, creativity, or other advantages to change the situation.
- *The problem is unsolvable:* You think the problem cannot be solved, because of rules or laws, complexity, lack of resources, or other constraints. Thus, even if you were capable, you conclude that the effort is futile.
- *The environment is unchangeable:* You think the systems, politics, or external forces are greater than any efforts you or others could possibly put forth now or in the future.

As you focus on any of these proven paths to feeling stuck, the chemicals in your brain create a self-reinforcing cycle that makes you feel even more helpless. This cycle can happen anywhere: in staff meetings where you are not being heard, when you are trying to learn a new skill, or when you are working with an uncooperative child. The more you explain your situation in one of these stuck ways, the more they become self-fulfilling prophecies.

In fact, if you continue to perceive that you are stuck and lack any choice, an excess of myelin, a substance that surrounds neurons and acts as an insulator, will ultimately build up in your brain and interfere with communication between its different regions. If this state continues, the brain can actually shrink in the areas related to controlling your emotions, metabolism, and memory.

All these negative feedback loops could sound quite dismal. But just as your brain can start down the path to stuck, it can just as easily find a more adaptive focus.

Your Brain With Options

The good news is that in the same way that feelings of helplessness can alter your brain chemistry in one direction, focusing on options can redirect your brain. The perception of having options triggers a different chemical chain reaction that alters your brain in a more useful way. And remarkably, you do not even have to act on those options to improve your situation. Just believing that you have them improves your ability to deal with demands and changes the chemicals in your brain.

Evidence of this observation includes research conducted by Martin Seligman, professor of psychology at the University of Pennsylvania. He showed that when people perceive a choice, they could better ignore an annoying distraction even if they did nothing to change the situation. In the experiment, the subjects had to perform a task while an annoying noise was distracting them. Those who were given a choice to turn off the noise out-performed those who did not have a choice, even though very few people ever bothered to turn off the noise. Just knowing they had the choice changed the way they were able to cope with their situation and get results!

When you believe you have even one option, your brain sends endorphins, enkephalins, and dopamine—three substances that together block pain, stimulate the immune system, provide energy, and give a sense of reward. This adaptive focus causes a flow of new chemicals, quiets down the amygdala, and kicks in the prefrontal cortex, with its problem-solving capabilities.

One of the most extreme examples of this principle of control comes from the prisoner-of-war camps during the Vietnam War. There, the prisoners were tortured, starved, and isolated. It was truly a living hell, and many prisoners found that to survive, they had to focus on choices they *could* control. They could choose to not eat, not cooperate, not move, or not talk. By creating options for themselves when none would ordinarily exist, they achieved a sense of power and the will to live.

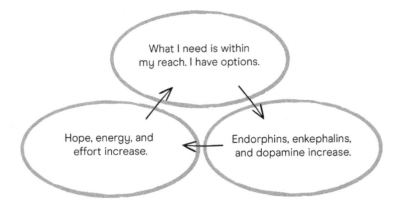

Fortunately, you are not likely to suffer in a prisoner-of-war camp. Yet sometimes, you can feel quite stuck attending a hostile meeting, trying to smooth a dysfunctional interaction, or facing an intimidating skill deficiency. You may not be able to change everything, but when you decide that you have options, this decision catalyzes a change in your brain chemistry and works to your advantage. Learning to increase your options gives you a new sense of autonomy and choice.

Learning to Find Options

You may already be good at creating options, or you may struggle with the concept. But in either case, you can improve your option-finding abilities. Jeff Dyer, whose innovation research we highlighted in the previous chapter, says that "creativity skills are not simply genetic traits endowed at birth, but that they can be developed."

This ability of normal people to learn to create new solutions has been validated in multiple twin studies where researchers have shown that although intelligence was largely genetic, creativity was much more influenced by desire, exploration, and environmental factors than by genetics. In other words, increasing your ability to create options and new ideas is learnable. You just need a little practice.

Three ways to improve your ability to create options are: creating an options mindset, building an options skill set, and developing an option-rich lifestyle. We will examine these approaches in detail.

Create an Options Mindset

Central to finding solutions when you are faced with difficult, painful, or impossible choices is having a default response that begins creating options and gets your brain chemicals flowing in the right direction. The NASA engineers had to believe that they could find a solution. Even though they did not know exactly what they would do, their mindset began with an assumption that an achievable option had to exist.

Having a core belief that an option exists to solve the problems in your pit of success gives you a reason to try. A key phrase that can create this mindset is this: "What I need is within my reach."

A Chinese aquarium applied this concept when a couple of its dolphins chewed the plastic off the edges of the pool and became deathly ill as the plastic filled their stomachs and prevented them from eating other food. The staff wished they could simply reach inside the animals' stomachs and grab the debris, but the distance from a dolphin's mouth to its stomach was too great, and any mechanical device would hurt the dolphins.

The staff decided the only way to reach the debris without harming the dolphins was to find one of the world's tallest humans, Bao Xishun, and have him reach into the creatures' mouths and grab the plastic. Bao traveled to Fushun, China, from Mongolia and, with his 3.5-foot arm, reached inside the dolphins and removed the plastic. What the aquarium staff had needed was ultimately within their reach, but they needed to reach outward for someone who could reach far enough.

When you repeat the phrase "What I need is within my reach" often, you encourage your brain chemicals to flow in the direction of autonomy and problem-solving. As a result, you are more likely to create options and take action.

Just like catastrophizing and assuming you have no control are habits, so is adopting the philosophy of "What I need is within my reach." This purposeful mindset can become a very liberating habit. It is like a muscle that can be strengthened through repeated exercise. As you repeatedly apply the phrase, it becomes part of your daily challenges.

- When things are not working out: "What I need is within in my reach."
- When things are breaking: "What I need is within in my reach."
- When you are behind: "What I need is within in my reach."
- When you do not know what to do: "What I need is within in my reach."
- When there appears to be no solution: "What I need is within in my reach."

Starting with the belief that what you need is within your reach frees your brain to find better options.

Build an Options Skill Set

In combination with a mindset for finding options, you can also increase your skill set for expanding options. The problem-solving methodology that follows provides proven techniques to help you generate options and find solutions. In short, the four key steps are these:

1. Define the problem.
2. Ask leading questions.
3. Magnify your resources and options.
4. Experiment.

Define the Problem

The most important action you can take to find better options is to define the problem. This point bears repeating. To find better options, *you must clearly define the problem.* The way you define a problem affects the direction you go and the quality of the solution you obtain.

An undefined problem, or seemingly impossible problem, causes the amygdala to activate and create tension and fear. Your brain feels lost. But by framing the problem clearly, you create a sense of order from the chaos and begin to take control.

The NASA team quickly defined the problem as getting the astronauts home alive by providing clean air. That definition of the problem allowed them to narrow their efforts.

No question is more critical to creating the right options than this, "What problem I am trying to solve?" By answering this question, you benefit in multiple ways:

- Focus on the real problem, not symptoms.
- Reduce anxiety, catastrophizing, distractions, and wasted efforts because you are naming the problem.
- Set the boundaries for your and others' efforts.
- Avoid preconceived answers.
- Focus your brain's energy.

The little extra time you take to define the problem will come back to you in the form of better and faster solutions.

Ask Leading Questions
Your brain likes doing one thing at a time. In fact, according to neuroscientist John Medina, "We are biologically incapable of processing attention-rich inputs simultaneously." This attribute becomes a great advantage when you are creating options to solve problems. When you ask yourself a question, your brain begins to search for the answer and shuts off other activities.

Asking a leading question will take priority over other activities such as catastrophizing, brooding, or feeling helpless. The brain literally has no room for these unhealthy activities as it searches for the answer to the purposeful question.

While many great questions can lead you to a solution, here are five to get you started:

1. What do I want to happen?
2. What do I wish I had?
3. What would be a second-best solution?
4. What small steps would get me closer to a solution?
5. If it were possible to solve this, what could happen?

Magnify Resources and Options
After the NASA support team members defined the problem and asked leading questions, they started looking at what resources were available. They needed to find a solution with the resources available to the astronauts. A resource can be anything you can access to achieve your goal. It could include a physical object, time, a knowledgeable colleague, your own skill, an idea, a previous piece of work, money, or even the air you breathe.

To magnify your options, use these three approaches to find the resources you need:

- *Existing resources:* Determine what you already have. You can increase, decrease, stop, or maintain your use of these existing resources.
- *Repurposed resources:* Take what you have, and use it in a new way (e.g., exchange an existing meeting time for a new purpose).
- *Acquired resources:* Reach beyond what you currently possess to bring in additional supplies, knowledge, funds, time, and skills.

The NASA team assessed what the astronauts had on board the spacecraft, repurposed these resources (hoses, socks, manual cover, etc.), and used a team of people thousands of miles away from the problem to save the astronauts' lives.

To magnify your resources, ask yourself these questions:

- What do I already have?
- How can I repurpose what I have for something that I wish I had?
- How can I get more time, money, people, materials, computing power, supplies, or data beyond what I now have?
- Who can I call on for help?

You always have more resources than you initially assume. The resources you need are within your reach. But you do need to reach!

Experiment

Once you find an option, you need to try it out. The NASA team made multiple attempts before providing their solution to the astronauts. Even though the clock was ticking, they experimented with different approaches to solving the problem. Discovering that the plastic bags ripped when they first tried to create the filter, the engineers adjusted their approach quickly, adding the cardboard manual cover to strengthen the bags. Their rapid prototyping and quick mistakes allowed them to create something that saved lives.

Taking action with your new options should be treated as an experiment, not a test. In an experiment, the goal is to see what will happen. There is no judgment about right or wrong. The idea simply worked or did not work. In contrast, if you treat the option as a test of your intelligence or competence, then the outcome can be quite punishing. Everything you try becomes a potential threat.

It often takes multiple experiments to find the right combination of ingredients to make things work. Here are a few ways that help you experiment:

- Act quickly.
- Try small steps.
- Attempt in low-risk environments, if possible.
- Ask others about your options before trying.
- Add, combine, and adjust your options.
- Get fast feedback.
- Try the next option.

Sometimes your experimenting will tell you that you need to go back and find other options. That is OK. You will find a solution. What you need is within your reach.

Develop an Options Lifestyle

The ability to create options and solve problems is enhanced by your lifestyle—what you study, the people you interact with, and the experiences you collect. The character Angus MacGyver, of the eponymous TV series *MacGyver*, was a distinct kind of hero who exemplified the options-rich lifestyle to the extreme. Instead of using guns, superpowers, or money to save the day, he was famous for his ability to come up with an endless array of options to escape the most dangerous situations.

The foundation for his ingenuity came from a life filled with education, experiences, and a few key supplies he always seemed to carry. Here is a partial list of why MacGyver was so good:

- Had degrees in physics and chemistry
- Spoke seven languages
- Learned bomb deactivation skills in military service
- Gained hang gliding, rock climbing, parachuting, self-defense, and outdoor survival skills
- Knew Morse code and maritime flag signals
- Played hockey, raced cars, painted, and played guitar
- Had a broad network of people
- Carried a Swiss Army knife
- Often had duct tape, chewing gum, paper clips, matches, and flashlight in his pocket
- Kept a toolbox in his Jeep

No wonder MacGyver could do anything; he had so much to draw from! And although the character is fictional, the lesson is real: more knowledge, more experience, and a set of tools give you more ways to create options.

You do not, however, need degrees in physics and chemistry to develop a lifestyle aligned with creating options. You can develop your options lifestyle through these simple practices:

- Take classes on diverse topics.
- Watch how-to YouTube videos.
- Subscribe to different magazines.
- Read books on various topics.
- Talk to people with different viewpoints and skill sets.
- Travel.
- Intentionally develop a new expertise.
- Take a new road to work.
- Try a new project, hobby, or activity.

You can also keep a toolbox in your house and car, and you may even choose to carry a Swiss Army knife, duct tape, and chewing gum in your pocket.

Your company can also develop an options lifestyle as you create a culture that values appropriate risk-taking and learning. Some companies create teams that work on targeted projects that offer ways to learn without becoming embroiled in bureaucracy or creating risk to the core business. Lockheed Martin was the originator of this concept back in the 1940s, with its Skunk Works, a less formal, more exploratory program in the company.

Much later, Google also adapted a broader approach to exploring options. The company gives its employees a percentage of their workweek to explore creative ideas on work time. Some of the projects work, and some do not. But the key is that they create a mindset within the organization for exploring and learning.

You and your company do not need to be MacGyver to find options for the next pit of success you face. You can start small and add to your foundation over time. When you combine your life experiences with an options skill set and an options mindset, you will find that you can create possibilities for anything.

Creating Better Options

The engineers at NASA were able to make something out of nothing because they brought knowledge, experiences, and a mindset that allowed them to find options. To find a solution, their problem-solving brains focused on defining the problem and discovering how they could use their limited resources in entirely new ways.

Your brain will work to your advantage when you focus on finding options. Developing options is not some magical skill that only a few are gifted with. It is learnable. When you start looking for options, you will find new ways to navigate your pit of success. As you explore options, you will discover that what you need is truly within your reach.

Key Ideas

- Your brain is sensitive to how you explain your situation. Describing your condition with words like *incapable*, *unsolvable*, and *unchangeable* increases feelings of helplessness at a neural level and reduces your willingness to try. Conversely, a mindset that assumes there is some type of solution increases hope and ways to find more options.

- Research shows that the skill of developing options is something you can learn.

- Expand your options mindset by defining situations confidently: "What I need is within my reach."

- Develop an options skill set by studying problem-solving, creativity, and improvisation.

- Try this problem-solving method to expand options and find solutions:
  1. Define the problem: "What problem am I trying to solve?"
  2. Ask leading questions: "What do I want to happen?"
  3. Magnify your resources and options:
     - Assess: "What do I already have?"
     - Repurpose: "How can I use what I have in new ways?"
     - Expand: "How can I add resources (time, materials, skills, funding, people, etc.)?"
  4. Experiment: "How can I quickly discover if my option will work?"

- Develop an options lifestyle by asking yourself, "How can I routinely add experiences, knowledge, and tools to my life?"

- The need for options applies equally to individuals, teams, departments, and companies. Every difficult situation gives you limited resources and excess demands that require new options and innovations to navigate your pit of success.

CHAPTER 7

Slow Down to Speed Up

On lap 175 of the Daytona 500 NASCAR race, a yellow flag went up and Rusty Wallace—in the number one position in the race—had to decide whether to pull off for a pit stop to get new tires. At risk was over $3.0 million in prize money and awards. If Rusty stopped for those 11.5 seconds, the new tires would give him extra grip and perhaps allow him to make aggressive moves to maintain his lead. If he kept the worn tires, he would maintain his lead position while others took a pit stop, but he would be less nimble and potentially need to slow down in the last crucial minutes of the race. He and his crew chief decided that the current tires seemed to be performing well enough and that Rusty should keep racing without a break.

Competitor Jeff Gordon, following close behind on the track, chose to come in for new tires and risk the 11.5 seconds. During the next 25 laps, Jeff methodically gained ground against Rusty and took the lead. Rusty continued to fight for a lead position, but he just could not maintain it. He fell further and further back until, by the end of the race, he finished in eighth place, despite having led the race for 104 laps. Jeff had only led for 17 laps.

Over the years, the pit-stop strategy has become one of the most important features in the success or failure of a driver. Drivers pull in for a mere 11 to 13 seconds for fuel, tires, and the repair of mechanical problems, hoping to gain an edge to win the race. Race teams regularly debate "Keep going or replenish?" It is a difficult debate that everyone faces on and off the track.

(Note: A pit stop and the pit of success share the word *pit*. But the words do not share the same definition. A pit stop is a break to replenish or fix something, while the pit of success represents the demands you must navigate to achieve your next level of expertise.)

Arguing with Yourself

Unfortunately, I (Dave) have personally lost this debate in my own race back and forth between home and the airport. Many years ago, a red warning light briefly lit up on my dashboard, indicating the oil was low. The light turned off so soon, I promptly forgot about it. When it came on again a few days later, I headed out to get oil, but it was too late. My engine seized up and I had to be towed. The mechanic told me that I needed a new engine, but he recommended just buying a new car.

It is easy to rush from place to place, ignoring the red warning lights and other quiet messages, and to just continue driving. The signal to stop is often so subtle, and your race so critical, that it is hard to find the time to rest and renew. In the midst of your race, making space for a little oil, tires, rest for your eyes, or a short walk can all seem like luxuries that you cannot possibly do now but hope to do someday, when you have the time and energy for it.

Whether you are driving a race car, leading a team at work, working on a test, parenting, caring for sick parents, volunteering, learning a new skill, or releasing a product, you face the same nagging question: "Can I really take the time to stop, or do I just keep going and hope I make it?"

This is a difficult question to answer. You have legitimate reasons to keep going, even though your brain and body may need rest. You and your brain are having a heated debate.

Your Brain's Arguments

Your brain is designed to work hard. Yet, your brain is also quite demanding. It needs two-thirds of the glucose you consume and twenty percent of the oxygen you breathe. To continue operating and providing for your needs, your brain requires many resources:

- Glucose
- Oxygen
- Water
- Nutrients
- Stimulus
- Rest

These resources are like the oil and gas in your car. Without them, performance declines or stops. In fact, when you lack any of these, your cognitive functioning can decline as though your IQ had dropped. An imbalance in any of your brain's basic needs can lead to a decrease in your problem-solving aptitude, creativity, memory, empathy, and decision-making ability.

For example, you have probably experienced the "brain fog" from a lack of sleep that makes you less effective and less present. Sleep is so critical that just fifteen minutes less sleep than usual can decrease your functional IQ and reduce your performance on a test. Similarly, a mere one or two percent drop in hydration level decreases your alertness and concentration, even though you usually do not feel thirsty at that point.

Your brain cannot be fooled, even when you are. When you ignore the basics, you and your results pay a price. One famous case of ignoring your brain comes from Arianna Huffington, the cofounder of the *Huffington Post* news site. From 2005 to 2007, Arianna worked eighteen-hour days traveling nationally and internationally. She rarely got enough rest and was on her phone as soon as she woke up.

Then in a moment, her life changed. Arianna collapsed in her home office and was found unconscious, her head lying in a pool of blood. Up until then, she had lived by a creed of nonstop hard work and always being on. Her doctor told her she would need to make serious changes to her lifestyle, or she would likely experience a similar episode of passing out. Reluctantly she began to change.

For too long, Arianna had ignored the basics and did not recognize the warning signs. But her brain and body would not be tricked. She had depleted her reserves, and the good she had wanted to do was interrupted. Her brain and body did not consider how noble her cause was or how ambitious her dreams; they just knew they were depleted.

Fortunately, Arianna recovered. She stepped down from her role at the *Huffington Post* and now writes and speaks to inspire people to quit ignoring their needs just because they like their job or because the culture expects them to work more hours. She decided she could ultimately give more if she slowed down.

The brain's argument is simple: "Take care of me, or I cannot take care of you." While your brain is happy to give its all to your challenges, it is simply unable to continue working in a state of deprivation. You cannot ignore the neuroscience without paying a price and becoming depleted. The brain's logic to win the argument is strong, yet so often we still ignore these basic needs.

Your Competing Arguments

You already know that you probably need a better diet, more exercise, and rest, but simply knowing these will rarely produce long-term change. Competing against your knowledge of the needs of the brain are three strong arguments: "I can't stop," "I shouldn't stop," and "I don't want to stop."

Imagine how Arianna battled these arguments to ignore her brain's need for sleep and nutrition. "I can't take a break; I won't get the funding we need. I shouldn't rest—this is what successful people do. I don't want to stop; I love the feeling and rush of these challenges."

These challenges to your brain's needs are based on real constraints, guilt and shame, and a bias for action. As you identify which arguments you rely on, you can overcome the impact they have on you.

Real Constraints ("I Can't Stop")

You are not just imaging that things are hard and that you have lots to do. You are facing real limitations and pressures that have actual consequences. The pit of success you face has demands that do not allow you to just leave for Hawaii when the pressure boils over and deadlines approach. There are significant things that truly *are* out of your control. You must pay the bills, deal with someone's bad behavior, finish the task, meet your deadlines, and feed your family.

Throughout your life, you face situations, responsibilities, and other circumstances that make it very difficult to keep your brain running at optimal capacity. Sometimes, getting eight hours of sleep is nearly impossible, because you have to meet the urgent demands piling up in front of you. The constraints are real; you have no magic wand to make them go away.

However, real constraints are vastly different from having no control. It is not realistic to *not* feed your baby, to ignore the water flooding your home, or to miss a critical deadline. But within each demand is always something you can control. You can choose to pause for a minute during the chaos. You can choose to go to bed seven minutes earlier. You can choose to breathe peacefully while you take care of the baby with your eyes closed.

You do not care for the brain in the absence of demands and constraints; you nurture yourself in the midst of them. Once you acknowledge your constraints, you are free to explore options for what you can control.

Guilt and Shame ("I Shouldn't Stop")

You may believe in taking a break, but you may also feel that doing so makes you irresponsible or selfish. This argument can come from a combination of guilt and shame.

Guilt, in its best form, nudges you to be honest, stand for good, and be responsible. This "healthy" guilt from parents, school, and culture gives you a conscience, helps you develop empathy, and creates a moral compass. You can feel guilty about a mistake, change your actions, and then do better in the future.

Shame, however, would propose that you hold yourself forever captive by dwelling on mistakes, beating yourself up for putting demands on others, or despising yourself for not being as smart as people expect you to be. Despite your wanting to take time for your needs, shame says that you are unworthy or undeserving. You can even feel shame about feeling shame or guilt.

When you realize, however, that you are good enough *with* your imperfections, mistakes, and doubts, you can give your brain what it needs. Taking care of your brain is not about waiting until you arrive at some future perfect state. Remember, you are not in your current situation because you have all the answers. You are there because you are capable enough to find the answers you seek. It is that simple—you are not supposed to have it figured out yet.

Bias for Action ("I Don't Want to Stop")

You might find that you naturally keep going to achieve the next thing on your list and that you routinely skip pit stops. This habit may be genetic—or it may have been learned—but the joy of just getting one more thing done drives you to keep going. Your brain has practiced this non-stop path so consistently that you seek out the dopamine hits that produce a sense of gratification with each item completed. It is exciting, fun, and satisfying to get things done.

This drive keeps you going. There is always more to do: more impact, more tasks, more to give, more money to make, and more dopamine to enjoy. No matter how many things you do, it is never enough. Never! It is like an addiction. However, despite your passion for more, your brain and body keep a running total on what you do for them—and fail to do for them. Even if you can fool yourself into believing you do not need to work differently, you cannot fool your brain and body. Your noble cause does not change the impact to your brain, your health, your loved ones, or your results.

Bernie, a sales manager, was a bias-for-action type of guy. He had big goals and was driven to get everything done on his to-do list. But he soon found that no matter how much he did, he was still behind, and the pace was taking a toll on him. He was so chained to his to-do list that he could not stop, yet he was never satisfied. He always had to do more.

Fortunately, a colleague helped him reframe his situation by suggesting that Bernie would have more freedom and results if he focused on who he wanted to *be* rather than what he had to *do*. For Bernie, this revelation was a turning point. His to-do list became his ally rather than his master. He went on to lead global business units and become a company president—*all while taking care of himself.*

All this talk of taking care of yourself may cause you to worry that you will end up sitting around doing nothing and expecting others to do your share of the work. That is not going to happen for one simple reason: such a hands-off approach is not who you are! Just because you take care of your brain does not mean you become irresponsible. In fact, as you choose to care for your brain, you increase the amount of control in your life and are better able to give more. See "An Unscientific but Useful Depletion Quiz" to assess your current arguments.

The powerful arguments of real constraints, guilt and shame, and a bias for action do not have to override the needs of your brain. You can take care of yourself and still win your race. In fact, you may find that you can achieve great things without even feeling like you are in a race.

What is your argument?

An Unscientific but Useful Depletion Quiz

What is your argument for staying depleted?
Rate the following statements, using a five-point scale,
where 1 = "Not like me" and 5 = A lot like me."

I can't stop, because ...
___ I will get punished.
___ I will be farther behind or miss out.
___ There are too many constraints.

I shouldn't stop, because ...
___ only lazy people take breaks.
___ others will suffer.
___ I don't deserve it.

I don't want to stop, because ...
___ I like getting one more thing done.
___ I like the adrenaline.
___ I just have a bias for action.

Scoring: If you total more than 10 points in any category, you probably find it easy to use these arguments as solid justification for ignoring the needs of your brain and for skipping any pit stops. If you have more than 10 points in several categories, then you probably find it easy to ignore almost all prompts to take a pit stop.

How to Slow Down to Speed Up

Embedded in the above arguments is the belief that your present self lacks enough space, time, or resources for taking care of yourself. Real constraints, shame, and a bias for action contend that you presently do not have time to solve your problem. Instead, they argue that your future self will make better decisions than your present self will. Your future self will eat better, exercise more, rest more, save more, and have more time. You name it, the belief is that your future self will be in a much better position to make the changes you want in life. The unfortunate reality is that the idea of a future self is just a summation of all your present selves, day after day, decision after decision.

You may find your present self using wishful phrases like these:

- If only …
- Someday I'll …
- When things are …
- After this one, I'll …
- When I have__, I can …

These phrases (and the behaviors they drive) maintain a depletion loop. They help you believe that if only you were not facing this pit of success, then you would be able to take care of yourself. When things are less hurried, the arguments contend, you will have time to breathe. When you have more experience, you will have time for yourself and your family. After you finish just one more call, task, or project, you will have more space, time, or energy.

Getting off the depletion loop and winning your debate against these unhelpful arguments means finding space for yourself *while* you are facing demands. You create your future today by developing a future-friendly mindset and mastering the moments.

Create a Future-Friendly Mindset

Your mindset is the narrative you repeat to yourself every day in the good moments and the bad. It is what you believe about the past, this moment, and the future, and it determines your choices. A future-friendly mindset looks at the big picture and asks, "Is the way I am racing really helping me get there faster?" and "Is the way I believe and behave today taking care of both my current and my future self?" You can create such a mindset by checking your current beliefs, discovering the facts, and updating your mindset accordingly.

Check Your Current Mindset

Your genetic predispositions, your experiences, and the environment you grew up in have influenced your mindset and how you approach work and life. For example, families and the rest of society commonly advocate a "work hard and be tough" message. This important lesson is taught through generational stories of relatives who worked hard (and those who did not) and cultural messages of what hard work and toughness look like.

The training known as Hell Week for U.S. Navy SEALs, U.S. Marines, and U.S. Army Rangers is one place that hard work and toughness are showcased. These elite military personnel are pushed to their limits through extreme weather, dehydration, muscle fatigue, tear gas, and five days without sleep. It is a grueling experience designed to develop the "best of the best" and let them know the price they may have to pay to succeed. The messages to be learned are clear: hard work is required to succeed, you are more capable and tougher than you imagine, and you must work as a team to succeed.

These military specialists deserve great respect for their commitment and sacrifice. However, if you are not careful, these depictions of "work hard and be tough" can also include unintended messages about life and work. Consider some of these misconceptions:

- If you are hurting and suffering, then you are on the right path.
- If you are taking abuse, then you are worthy.
- If you have achieved a high level of fatigue today, then you have done something noble.
- If you rest, you are weak.

These unintentional messages are not the full story of the military elite. When they go on real missions, the deprivation and demands of training are no longer the model for success. These on-the-job warriors must live a very brain-friendly life.

Former Army Ranger Matthew Steele knew what it meant to be tough but also knew that merely being tough was not enough for peak performance. He explains, "When we were out on a mission for several days, I kept focusing on the basics. I reminded my team to hydrate, take care of their nutrition, and make sure they did not push so hard getting to the objective that they would have no juice left when they arrived. Rest and replenishment were as important as speed. I could not afford to have anyone who was not mentally alert. If they were not focused, people died." As a leader in life-and-death situations, Matthew could not risk a unilateral focus of only toughness for his team; he needed them to be healthy and fully alert.

Checking your mindset for mixed or out-of-date messages frees you from patterns that are not serving you. After all, if you are going to repeat a story to yourself, make sure it gives you what you need. To check your mindset, consider these questions:

- What is the story I tell myself about needing to work more or harder?
- What, if any, unintended messages are mixed in with the healthy messages?
- Do I need to question any of my conclusions about how I approach my work?
- How future-friendly is my current mindset?

Discover the Facts

Creating a future-friendly mindset is easier when you have solid research to debunk any out-of-date conclusions about taking a break. When you know that your new choices are based on relevant facts, it is easier to make space for your brain's needs.

Research from the early 2000s has redefined what we know about succeeding when the pressure is on. Consider this workplace study that examined whether constantly working is the path to success.

In the fast-paced and high-demand world of management consulting, working long hours at Boston Consulting Group (BCG) is something that consultants both brag about and resent. They are assigned to projects with seventy- to eighty-hour workweeks on the road and are expected to generate immediate and high-quality responses to client requests.

Historically, the brutal schedule was accepted as a necessary part of success. However, Leslie Perlow, professor of leadership at Harvard Business School, convinced BCG to run an experiment with five consultants who would dedicate one day a week to fully break from the demands of their project. No emails. No calls. No planning. Just take a break from the demands of the job. The practice was hard to embrace, but the consultants gradually learned to take time to fully break away from work.

After just five months of this consistent planned time off, the results made a clear and compelling case that taking a break from the treadmill of consulting paid off big. The benefits included the following:

- Value delivery increased by 9.4 percent.
- Job satisfaction increased by 10.4 percent.
- Open team communications increased by 12.5 percent.
- Work/life balance increased by 16.3 percent.

The group learned to work together more effectively and to support one another's time off. The experiment's impact was so successful that it was rolled out to other teams across BCG.

In summarizing the success of the new approach, the CEO said that planned time off "not only enhance[d] work-life balance, making careers sustainable, but also improved client value delivery, consultant development, business service team effectiveness, and overall case experience." Creating time for people to disconnect paid off for the individual, the team, and the company.

Similar results have been found in a variety of studies that show significant benefits in accuracy, quality, safety, problem-solving, decision-making, and promotions when people take a break, make time to stretch, change their focus, go for a walk, take a vacation, or simply breathe.

The research does not say you should not work hard. On the other hand, it does clearly demonstrate that taking time for your brain during hard work is not something to feel guilty about. Taking a break is something that benefits you and the greater good—at home and at work. Creating space is not a selfish luxury; it is a performance advantage.

Update Your Mindset

A future-friendly mindset is something you create and re-create throughout your life. By assessing your current mindset and adding new information, you can be intentional about what you tell yourself and what actions you take.

Consider these questions to start updating your mindset:

1. What am I currently doing to help myself take care of my brain? Is there anything that used to work that is not working anymore?
2. What things or situations tend to hold me back from taking care of my needs (deadlines, guilt or shame, fear, others' needs, adrenaline, etc.)?
3. What advice would my future self give me about my current situation? What would someone who genuinely wants the best for me recommend doing to better take care of my needs? What mindset would I like to grow into (e.g., doing something differently, doing more, doing less, balancing my needs and others', focusing on who I am instead of what I need to do)?
4. What help, if any, do I need (e.g., from friends, family members, counselors, coaches, and colleagues)?

Most people are overly optimistic that their future selves will somehow have more time and resources to fix their problems, but it is your current self that finds solutions. Challenging out-of-date beliefs and trying new behaviors can make your new mindset a reality and help you achieve more.

Remember, you do not have to be good at taking a break at first. As simple as it sounds, learning to take a break is a new skill that will take some practice. Your learning curve may be slower than you wish, but small steps repeated will make it easier for you to take breaks.

Master the Moments

Everything you experience in life is wrapped up in moments. Some moments are longer than others, but life is a string of many moments. While you may not be able to control an entire day, an hour, or sometimes even five minutes, you do have significant influence within the moments of your pit of success.

At this very instant, you could yell, laugh, turn your head, stand up, lie down, start walking, open your mouth, sing, yawn, pick up the phone, hold your breath, read, close your eyes, ponder, breathe slowly, write, smile, or attempt to wiggle your ears. You have so many options for how you use this moment. In the midst of meetings, calls, studying, typing, emails, errands, family, and children, there are thousands of moments that you can control.

What you believe about these segments of time and how you treat them determine your ability to get through your pit of success without burning out. To master your moments, ask yourself these three questions: "What am I feeling?" "What do I need?" and "What do I want to do about it?"

What Am I Feeling?

In the pit of success, it is normal to feel that you are in over your head, not good enough, and exhausted. You are doing things you have little experience doing, and your brain is having to work overtime. These demands create an array of feelings: fatigue, guilt, shame, pressure, boredom, helplessness, joy, excitement, loneliness, stiffness, confusion, hurt, fear, anger, tension, and others.

Naming what you are feeling helps you take control of your

situation. Remember, the act of verbalizing your feelings shifts the thought from the amygdala to the prefrontal cortex. Taking a moment to ask, "What am I feeling?" gives you power to act so that you can decide what to do. Even if you cannot label the feeling, simply acknowledging, "I don't know what I feel right now," is a way to empower yourself to find what you need.

What Do I Need?

When you know what you feel and pause to ask, "What do I need?" you create space to find the options you need to care for your brain and yourself. In addition to the familiar good choices of rest, stretch, eat better, and get moving, you have unlimited ways to master the moment. You can connect with others, find some quiet time, get nourishment, seek out a challenge, get moving, clarify your situation, or explore the beauty around you (see Appendix C, "Ninety-Nine Ways to Take Care of Yourself").

Consider these examples of people we have worked with:

- A new hire overwhelmed with all he had to learn in the first year of the job made a habit of a weekly bike ride. It was one of his favorite things, and it always seemed to rebalance him after a week of stress and confusion.
- A company president busy in back-to-back meetings got burned-out during the day and started asking some of his appointments if they could go for a walk while they talked. He gained energy, and people felt at ease.
- A middle manager overwhelmed with learning to develop a more strategic focus decided that she needed someone else to do some of the work. She delegated some of her tasks and was able to pay more attention to company strategy.

- A leader with a demanding international travel schedule found the respite she needed by creating an evening ritual of sparkling water with lemon (or lime) at the end of her twelve-hour day. The habit helped her pause and renew, and anywhere she went in the world, she could always find her moment. The relaxing ritual gave her a sense of control.

By pausing and exploring what you really need, you can increase the value of any moment you have in front of you. Your simple actions create a sense of control and develop a future-friendly mindset.

One word of caution as you ask what you need: there are also counterfeit moment fillers. These fake deposits include grabbing caffeine when you really need to rest your eyes for ten minutes, scrolling on your phone when you really need a walk around the park, finishing one more email when you need to call it a day, or watching another TV episode when you need to sleep. These practices may not be inherently bad, but they often fail to truly replenish you. Taking time to ask yourself, "Is this *really* what I need in this moment?" gives you a path to do what you most need. As you practice asking and listening, you get better at recognizing your true needs and doing what matters the most.

What Do I Want to Do About It?

Asking yourself, "What do I want to do about it?" is a way to gain power over the demands you meet every day. When you intentionally choose to act or not act, you tell your brain that you are in charge. And your brain loves autonomy. Just knowing that you are in charge and choosing not to act is sometimes enough to give you the energy you need. When you do choose to act, taking small steps is the most predictable path to find what you need.

B. J. Fogg, the founder of Persuasive Technology Lab (renamed the Behavior Design Lab in late 2019) at Stanford, is a big advocate of small. Fogg is called "the millionaire maker" because of the successful Silicon Valley entrepreneurs and engineers who have passed through his laboratory at Stanford. The secret to his results? Think really small! Fogg's research has shown that the smaller your action, the more likely you are to achieve your goal. His advice for big changes is simple: "Pick a small step ... a step so tiny, you'll think it's ridiculous."

This power of applying a ridiculously small change has been documented in the hospital operating room, where surgeons are required to stand for hours in a static posture with their hands and arms in the *sterile field*—the area that surrounds the incision and is kept relatively free of microorganisms through certain protocols.

The safety procedure requirements, along with the intensive nature of surgery, create significant physical and mental stress for the surgeons. In these life-and-death situations, you can imagine a surgeon saying, "I can't take a break; it will prolong the surgery and put the patient at risk. A break will also make all the team stay here longer. I don't want to stop; I just need to get done." With this mindset, however, surgeons routinely reported fatigue, impairment, injuries, patient risks, and career longevity issues.

To improve the situation, researchers at the Mayo Clinic introduced a future-friendly intervention that asked sixty-one surgeons to pause during surgery for less than a minute and do three simple actions:

- Stand up tall
- Take a deep breath
- Turn their head to the right or left

The results were significant. By taking this intentional micro-break every twenty minutes throughout a procedure, surgeons reported less post-surgery pain in their neck, lower back, shoulders, upper back, wrists, hands, knees, and ankles. Additionally, the majority of surgeons reported improved physical performance, and 38 percent described increased mental focus.

Sometimes, especially when you cannot get exactly what you want in the heat of a pit of success, you need to find the next-best thing. You may not have the time for a fifteen-minute break, but you can close your eyes for a minute. You may not have time for a bike ride, but you can go on a short walk or listen to refreshing music. You may not be able to quit for the day, but you can ask for help or take a moment to breathe.

You always have some small option that is better than doing nothing. Each small action makes a deposit, and a series of small deposits creates a reservoir. When you choose to take a small action, you become the master of your moments, and your brain loves you.

Winning the Argument

Taking time for yourself is not an extravagance, a guilty pleasure, or a backup plan. Winning the argument is about creating space for your brain's needs as a necessity for navigating your pit of success. Doing so gives you a competitive advantage.

Like any new habit, slowing down to speed up is learned over time with small efforts. You will not always do it perfectly. Some days, you will be better at it than others, but small daily efforts will create a more future-friendly lifestyle that both takes care of your needs and helps you excel at your current task.

Key Ideas

- Even race car drivers need to stop and replenish their resources to maintain a competitive edge.

- Everyone faces an internal debate when they encounter a pit of success: "Can I really succeed if take care of myself?" Fortunately, the answer is yes.

- You cannot fool your brain. It gets depleted without adequate water, glucose and other nutrients, oxygen, stimuli, and rest. When it is depleted, your IQ, memory, decision-making and problem-solving abilities, creativity, accuracy, and hope decline. The connection between your mental performance and your brain's health is simple neuroscience.

- A focus on constraints, shame, or a bias for action may be depleting your brain. Interrupting these arguments can help you make space within the real constraints you have.

- Research studies across different disciplines have proven that taking time for small breaks, nourishment, and vacations increases your accuracy, creativity, productivity, and other results. Taking this time also increases job satisfaction, the likelihood of being promoted, and employee retention.

- A future-friendly mindset looks beyond the tasks and focuses on the bigger purpose. Your future self will be grateful for the small actions that your present self takes in the midst of demands.

- You can master the moments by asking yourself, "What am I feeling?," "What do I need now?," and "What do I want to do about it?"

- Beware of fake deposits that take up time, rob you of energy, and continue to deplete the brain.
- The small actions you take each day can build habits that renew.

CHAPTER 8

Adapt, Succeed, and Repeat

Whether your pit creates doubt, frustration, or excitement, you now possess a set of principles and tools that can be applied in many situations to reduce your burdens, give you more control, and increase your ability to succeed. Identifying the right next step is not about having a perfect plan. Instead, choosing any one of the principles will get your brain going in the right direction.

When you start by acknowledging your *changeable brain*, you gain the energy to practice the building blocks so that you can ultimately achieve the hard things. When you focus on *embracing the pit*, you clarify your purpose and find greater meaning in doing what needs to be done. When you focus on *trading up*, you increase your influence on the things you can control. When you *make something from nothing*, you find better options. And when you start *slowing down to speed up*, you increase your energy.

The key is to start where you feel most comfortable starting, and if one approach does not work for your current situation, then another one surely will. You will learn from each path.

The Progressive Learning Cycle

Your brain will rewire itself with each pit of success you embrace. As you face obstacles, ambiguities, missteps, and decisions, you gain new expertise, which in turn makes you more able to navigate the next pit. Each demand can make you more and more capable. And while no one looks forward to demands, they can improve your ability to face any other challenge or adversity.

Without this cycle of growth, you would be the same person today that you were twenty years ago. Life would be a repeat of the same experiences limited by the same old responses.

Understanding this cycle will absolutely make it easier to embrace progressively more difficult demands, even though you still have to go through the learning process. You will still sometimes get lost and lack good answers; you must still interrupt the tendency to do things the old way; and, most importantly, you still have to practice new things. Fortunately, you are now doing these hard things with the knowledge that your brain will make the needed connection with some practice, and you will learn whatever you need to learn.

You no longer need to wonder if you are capable. You are. You no longer have to wonder why you are not getting it. You are not getting it because your brain has not done it enough to make the connection—yet. You no longer need to ask yourself, "Can I do these hard things?" You can meet these challenges, with the right building blocks, focus, and practice.

Everyone Faces the Pit

At any given moment, you may not feel as though you are learning, growing, or advancing. Some days, you might even feel like you are moving backward.

From your close vantage point, your current pit can feel deep and overwhelming, and you may wish you could just quit. No matter who you are, it is exhausting to redo things or to take such a long path. But you are in good company.

Even Michelangelo had to learn and adapt to successfully create the ceiling of the Sistine Chapel. When he was creating one of the larger compositions, he encountered a problem. The plaster had become overgrown with mold and it was destroying his beautiful creation.

There he was, sixty-five feet in the air, standing on scaffolding and looking at his masterpiece, which was being scarred. To move forward, he had to destroy his work because, unlike painting on a canvas, a fresco is not created by applying paint to a dry surface. Instead, dry-powder pigments are brushed onto wet plaster and become bonded as the plaster dries. Because of this, Michelangelo could not merely paint over his work. The fresco had to be chipped away and started again.

Despite Michelangelo's broad expertise, he was not exempt from the learning curve. He had to learn how to mix plaster and use it in a timely manner so that the mixture would not mold. He got better at using the fresco technique over time and went on to complete a masterpiece that has inspired thousands of tourists and followers for over five hundred years.

Michelangelo did not have everything figured out. He had to learn.

One of our favorite quotes is attributed to Michelangelo: "If people knew how hard I had to work to gain my mastery, it would not seem so wonderful at all." What Michelangelo describes in this statement applies to everyone who has gained any type of skill (musical, artistic, social, organizational, financial, technical, etc.). Initial abilities only give you a fast start, but the rest of the journey requires time, multiple steps, and hard work to find the next answers.

Every leader must figure out unpredictable problems that do not always go right the first time. In these moments of messiness, it can be easy to get channelized on the wrong thing at the wrong time and not see the bigger picture. But as you look at where you are going—the masterpiece you envision—and what you have already accomplished, the view is quite inspiring.

To reemphasize a point in Chapter 1, you are not in your job because you have all the answers; you are in your job to find answers. If you are willing to become temporarily incompetent and focus on gaining new expertise, you can continually adapt, succeed, and repeat. It is what you and your brain are designed to do.

What You Need Is Learnable

In closing, we share with you a personal text from a college student studying for her finals. In the message, she explains her deep frustrations with the pit of success:

> *I'm going to be really honest with you. Sometimes I do not like that you taught me about the pit of success. I mean, there are times I really just want to whine and complain because something is hard.*

> *I look at the problems I have to figure out and ask myself, "Why it is so difficult for me?" The easy answer I want to tell myself is, "I'm just not competent enough so it is impossible for me to learn this, and I should just quit trying." But because I understand the pit, I know that I have a changeable brain and I cannot legitimately have that argument, even though I wish I could.*
>
> *If I didn't know about the pit, I could just be sad about being dumb. But I know better than that ... and the thing is ... I just can't decide if I'm grateful or not for that knowledge as I struggle with this assignment because even though I want to quit, I know if I am willing to keep working and keep getting help I will figure this out.*

Indeed, we think she is right. By understanding the pit of success, you now know that what you need to accomplish is within your reach. You have a brain that can refocus, learn, and navigate truly hard things.

Yet, this knowledge can be painful because, sometimes, you do not want to hotwire your brain, embrace a pit, be resourceful or pragmatic, trade up, create options, or take care of yourself. Sometimes you simply feel tired, sad, overwhelmed, and ripped off, and you are not ready to embrace anything. Those feelings are normal—some days are like that, and that is really OK. What you need is learnable, and you will figure it out.

PART TWO:
REAL-WORLD APPLICATIONS

CHAPTER 9

Tips for Parents, Students, Managers, and Executives

The pit of success influences all aspects of life, including starting a new job, accepting a promotion, dealing with an organizational change, learning a new skill, receiving unwanted feedback, moving across the country, studying a language, making a career change, learning to parent, dealing with health challenges, and retiring. No matter what you are doing that involves change, you always have your current level of expertise that makes you feel secure as well as an unclear and difficult path that requires you to do things beyond your experience.

You will face the pit in varying shapes and sizes in each of your life roles. We have selected four roles—parent, college student, manager, and executive—and have provided a few additional tips on navigating the pit from these perspectives.

Parents

On a return trip home from Eastern Europe, I (Dave) arrived at the Budapest, Hungary, airport at 4 a.m. after just three hours of sleep. In my exhaustion, I incorrectly calculated the payment for the taxi and gave the driver $400 instead of $40. I did not realize my mistake until I was in the airport and the taxi was gone.

I then had to decide: do I tell my family about the mistake I made, or do I hide my embarrassment? On arriving home, I told my family of the error. I did not like admitting this massive mistake, but sharing the idea that mistakes are a part of life helps kids know they can navigate their own pits of success.

Helping children learn to manage the ups and down of life is every parent's challenge. Teaching children about pits you have faced is a natural way to normalize the learning process.

Additionally, the earlier-mentioned Carol Dweck, one of the foremost authorities on how parents can help their children develop their skills, has identified that teaching children to understand that they have a changeable brain is key to helping them learn. She has found that children as young as two years old respond to messages about doing hard things in healthy ways.

Here are a few additional suggestions based on Dweck's research and our experience:

- *Use "not yet"*: When a child is not understanding something, use the phrase, "You do not have it *yet*." This wording tells the child (and adults) that the task is learnable, that the person will eventually get it, but that they just have not yet figured it out.
- *Praise effort, not smarts:* Say things like "You worked hard on this" instead of "You are so smart."

- *Remind them that hard things take practice:* Remind children that they are not supposed to know how to do this thing at first. It will probably take multiple attempts before they begin to succeed.
- *Talk about how the brain can grow and change:* Encourage children with statements like these: "You have a brain that can change with practice. Look at the things you have already practiced and learned."
- *Share your learning curve:* As children see you do hard things and survive, they learn that they can, too. For example, "At work I had to learn a new computer program, and it took me more than three months. It was confusing. I called the help desk many times, and now I have it. My effort paid off."
- *Talk to yourself in gentle ways:* Your kindness to yourself when you are lost will help your children be kind themselves. Eliminate phrases like "Why aren't I getting this" or "What is the matter with me?" and replace them with "I wonder how I will learn this."

In addition, check to see if you are inadvertently sending any messages about being stuck. Children pick up on how you view your world, and they project it on their own lives.

College Students

For many people, college can be exciting as well as overwhelming, lonely, and hard. Many students sometimes find themselves asking, "Am I really good enough?" and "Do I belong here?" These concerns are normal. Yet, knowing what to expect in these difficult times has been shown to help students cope and perform better.

In one study, a group of first-generation college students was taught to expect that sometime in their first year of college, they would probably feel as if they did not belong and would be likely to face academic demands beyond their level of experience. Just knowing that these challenges were normal decreased the dropout rates among these students and improved their grade point averages. By understanding that college is a pit of success with doubts and challenges, the students found it easier to deal with the ups and downs.

Whether you are facing a pit of success in a class, in your social life, or with your new responsibilities, you will have an easier time achieving if you start with these two ideas. First, feeling lost and having to work harder than ever before are normal challenges. And second, the new capabilities you need to acquire are all learnable.

A few more tips for navigating college:

- *Get serious about believing you have a changeable brain:* When you believe your brain can adapt and learn, the challenge of difficult subjects becomes easier and more interesting. If you need more information about your changeable brain, do an internet search on neuroplasticity. You will find many videos that expand on your brain's ability to create new neural networks, to adapt, and to learn.

- *Redefine your definition of smart:* Smart is not about just getting answers immediately. Being smart starts with the knowledge that your brain and intelligence are developed through focus and repetition. New topics are only difficult because you do not yet have the neural pathways to facilitate the new thought or skill. When you build the pathway, you become smart.

- *Normalize the path of not knowing:* Being lost when starting a new topic, entering a new social setting, or experiencing a life change is normal. Because you have not faced the situation before, your brain lacks a pathway to draw from; you are not supposed to know how to do it yet. You will experience confusing times, but your changeable brain will adapt, and you will grow. It is just brain science.

- *Focus on purpose:* When things get tough, ask yourself why you are in school. What do you want to do in the future? What role does school play in that vision? If you do not yet know these answers, focus on finding purpose for the week, or even the day.

- *Ask for help:* Great performers, athletes, musicians, and executives get guidance to make themselves shine. Find a tutor or go to the learning lab. If that tutor is not a match, seek out another one. You do not have to do it all on your own.

- *Practice a few things for longer times:* Rather than studying the entire chapter, take a section, read it, take notes, and quiz yourself until you get it. Then move on.

- *Create a success list:* Take a moment to notice how your abilities to learn and perform grow each semester and year. You can read more, write faster and better, and manage more demands with each year of school. You may be surprised looking back at how your capacity to learn has improved over time.

- *Get some sleep:* Yes, sleep has been positively correlated with higher grades.

Managers

One of the main questions we get from managers is, "How do I help my people go through the pit?" Some of their people lack confidence, some do not want to try anything that requires effort, and some just really like what they are doing now. While no single answer will meet everyone's situation, here are some key approaches to start the process.

- *Share the normality of going through the pit:* Share ideas from Chapter 1, and if appropriate, tell about the times when you had to do things that you did not know how to do. The only caution here is to avoid making this about you and insisting your people should do it the way you did it. Many managers tell us that after they normalized the pit experience, a huge burden was lifted for the person the managers were talking with. Whether it was a new employee or a newly promoted executive, the person nevertheless felt relief.

- *Make the purpose or direction clear:* If people are clear on the big picture, they can better focus on what they need to do to get there. While this observation applies to all people, those who resist change and who really like operating at their current level of expertise especially need a compelling reason to let go and move forward into the pit. Clarity of purpose helps organizations get a bigger picture of their goals and individuals find their personal motivation.

- *Find assignments that create the right level of demand:* A core way you develop your people is through assignments that provide the right amount of challenge. Depending on where they are in their careers, your employees will need bigger or smaller challenges. The best leaders make appropriate demands that enable their people to grow, and these leaders support people as they navigate the pit.

- *Clarify the path to gaining new expertise:* Help define a development path, including the necessary steps for becoming competent in the new role. Make it clear what education, training, mentoring, coaching, and budget will be provided to support the person's journey. If something is not provided, clarify how you expect your people to gain the skill.

- *Find the building blocks:* Help your people identify one or two building blocks they should focus on first, rather than making them think that they need to learn everything now. Particularly for people who have significant doubts about their abilities, helping them find success in mastering one building block gives a foundation for change.

- *Focus on learning, not on missteps:* Not everyone does it right the first time. In a non-judgmental way, ask your people what they have learned from the missteps. As they explain, focus on really listening, not fixing. Express confidence in their ability to figure it out.

- *Rethink the number of projects:* If you want someone to grow, they need mental space and time. You will sometimes need to reduce the number or size of projects so that people have the time and space they need to navigate the new pit.

And remember, the pit of success is not something you punish people with or condemn them for not embracing. Telling someone, "Your problem is that you won't embrace the pit" will create more resistance than change. People will still struggle with leaving the comfort of their current expertise even when they understand the pit. Empathizing with the challenge of leaving one's current level of expertise and helping the person find meaning in moving to a new level is usually a better approach than condemning their struggle to embrace the pit. Your goal is to give hope.

Executives

All organizations struggle with holding on too long to processes, products, equipment, markets, clients, and beliefs that achieved their past success but that will not assure their future growth. Leading an entire organization, region, or function requires that you assess the pit of success that your organization must conquer and determine what areas your leaders must navigate to facilitate the next breakthrough.

Additionally, you must personally face your own pits of success because neither position nor experience prevents you from getting stuck in your current area of expertise and avoiding the need to adapt. In fact, sometimes the depth of your experience, the market risks, and the immediate pressures from your board of directors can encourage you to shun the changes that you and the business need to make.

Use the following table to distinguish between the changes that need to be made by you, your team, and your business. Be as detailed as you would like.

What Pits Need to Be Embraced?

You	Team	Business

You must help your people realize that what created success is not likely to maintain success in a changing market. Your good, talented people will agree with the need to change but will then return to their desks and do things the way they have always done them. It is just neuroscience: people are wired to repeat unless you create a way forward.

Helping your people embrace the pit individually and collectively is essential to making changes easier. You do not, however, want to weaponize the pit by hitting people over the head with it and punishing them for not changing as quickly as you think they should. Such a top-down approach rarely works.

Normalizing the human process of change and establishing a path for adoption is key to success. Appropriately sharing some of your own challenges of navigating pits in the past can help other people understand that what they need to do can be learned, despite their doubts.

For example, a company president at one high-potential leaders program I (Dave) was running told the group of executives and middle managers about his personal challenges in leading. Despite having been president at three organizations in the company, the only time he felt like he knew what was doing was when he was asked to return and lead one of the companies where he had been president a few years earlier. He explained that in the other leadership roles he had lacked familiarity with what needed to be done and experienced doubt, indecision, and confusion. His sharing of his challenges in going through the pit of success opened the door for other leaders to honestly discuss their own current challenges with one another. Executives set the tone for what other leaders will and will not share.

As an executive, the tips on the previous pages for managers apply equally to you and your team's development. Additionally, consider these strategic questions as you look to guide the organization, develop your leaders, and transform yourself.

1. What does winning (or success) look like in five years for my business, function, or product?
2. What are the major opportunities driving the business forward? What threats or challenges (external or internal) exist? Does the leadership team have a shared understanding of these drivers?
3. What capability (organizational, technological, financial, or human) got the organization here but needs to evolve (or stop being used) to achieve success in the future? What capabilities (new or existing) will be needed in five years, three years, or one year to achieve success?
4. What is most likely to keep the organization from acquiring the skills, processes, and strategy needed to be competitive in the next three years?
5. Does the organization have a passive or an intentional strategy for developing leaders to face the new challenges? What assignments, projects, and responsibilities need to be given so that they can grow?
6. What pit of success do I personally need to embrace to help the company succeed? Who can help me see what pit I need to embrace?
7. How ready are the people on my team to embrace the learning and changes needed to achieve success in the next five years? What do they need to understand about the market drivers and the pit of success?

As we have helped organizations answer these questions, we find that getting leaders to agree on these questions accelerates results for the business and develops a culture that evolves with changing markets.

CHAPTER 10

Four Real-Life Pits of Success

The following pages present four scenarios of people facing a pit of success. Although we provide possible recommendations on how they could start managing their demands, these are not the only actions they could take to navigate their pits of success. Use the table "Guide to Navigating the Pit of Success," and recommend what else you think they could do to make their pit easier to conquer.

Consider these scenarios:

- Same company, different country and work culture
- Fired twice
- Learning beyond one's core expertise
- "This is the way we have always done it."

Guide to Navigating the Pit of Success

Path	Tools

Hotwire your changeable brain	• Assess beliefs in changeable brain.
	  – Focus + repetition → change
	  – Different learning curves, same mastery
	  – Building blocks
	• Check for brain-friendly words.
	• Take small actions.

Embrace the pit	• Clarify purpose. • Redefine the betweenness. • Focus on discovery. • Narrow the scope. • Ask for help and feedback.

Trade up (and up)	• Check for limiting focuses: *stuck, should, hurt, fear,* or *justified.*
	• Interrupt the focus.
	• Name the feeling.
	• Replace the focus.
	  – What *is* happening?
	  – What is my purpose or direction?
	  – What can I learn or discover?
	  – What can I control or influence?
	  – What if I could do ___? What if I had ___?
	  – What am I grateful for?
	  – What small action can I take?

Make something from nothing	• Create an options mindset: What I need is within my reach.
	• Build an options skill set.
	  – Define the problem.
	  – Ask leading questions.
	  – Magnify resources and options.
	  – Experiment.
	• Develop an options lifestyle.

Slow down to speed up	• Develop a future-friendly mindset.
	  – What advice would my future self give me?
	  – What mindset would I like to grow into?
	  – What help, if any, do I need?
	• Master the moments.
	  – What am I feeling?
	  – What do I need?
	  – What do I want to do?

© 2020 Dave Jennings & Amy Leishman

Case 1: Same Company, Different Country and Work Culture

Judy, an engineering manager at a tech firm in Scotland, accepted a significant promotion at headquarters in Palo Alto, California. She, her husband, and their two kids moved to the United States with great excitement for an adventure in a new country with an awesome job.

Judy's work, however, has ended up being far more demanding than she expected. The pace of the office, the quantity of the work, and some difficult personalities make her day overwhelming. The managers above her are vague about priorities but are also demanding about high expectations. The transition from managing a team of ten to a team of fifty has been much more difficult than she anticipated. Despite working longer hours than she wants to work, she continually feels behind.

Compounding the problems, after six months, she and her husband decided it was time to get their U.S. driver's licenses. Unfortunately, however, both of them failed the test. Driving on the opposite side of the road while remembering all the rules of the road was incredibly daunting. They have rescheduled to take the test in a month.

Although the kids seem to be doing well in school, her husband has not found a job as easily as they had assumed. The job search support that the company promised has not been adequate.

Judy enjoys nature, bike riding, and drives (using her British license) through the mountains. But most of her off-work time is spent shuttling to and from her children's activities with her husband. She comes home from work exhausted almost every day and wonders if this move was such a good idea for her and her family.

How Judy Could Navigate Her Pit of Success

- **Hotwire her changeable brain:** Judy could ask herself if she believes that she can learn what she needs to know. She could also consider the words she is using to describe her situation and replace ineffective words. She and her husband may want to spend more time reading the drivers' handbook or get a tutor.

- **Embrace the pit:** Judy could benefit from redefining the betweenness that she and her family are experiencing. She could also review the purpose that brought her to this job. She could identify the steps involved in uncovering what she needs to learn, and she could notice what she has already learned. Instead of trying to leap across the pit, she should focus on a few things she wants to get good at. She might ask for some insight from people she trusts on how to deal with the demands and the difficult people.

- **Trade up (and up):** Judy may be overly focused on *stuck*, *should*, or *fear*. She could start interrupting her limiting thoughts with a question or a walk. She could also focus on purpose and identify the things she can control or influence.

- **Make something from nothing:** By starting to look for things within her reach that she can use, Judy could make the situation easier. She should define the problem she is trying to solve and create more options.

- **Slow down to speed up:** Judy might assess her mindset to see if any attitudes are out-of-date. She could take small breaks at work during the day by walking around the building or just finding a place to shut her eyes for a few minutes. Planned weekend trips to forested areas that she loves could also help. She should learn to say no to tasks outside her responsibilities.

Case 2: Fired Twice

A year and a half ago, Mark was fired from his job because his manager did not think that Mark was doing a good-enough job. Mark was never really sure what this criticism meant, but he found a job at an innovative start-up just a month later. Unfortunately, after one year, he was laid off from the new company. He was doing quite well at this company, but financial troubles had caused the company to let go of him and others—those with the shortest tenure.

Mark has just started a new job a month ago as an entry-level adviser. His work regularly requires him to face people whose experience, position, and expectations he finds intimidating. Although he has knowledge in the field, he feels much less experienced than the people he is supposed to be giving advice to. He must understand many types of companies, and people seem to question just how good he can be, given his age and experience level. They do not say anything specific, but their tone implies doubt.

In client meetings, he feels as if he must prove himself at every turn. He often wonders if he is not good enough for the role and if this new job could end like the others. Mark is afraid he may not make it and is always telling himself he should be better than he is.

Mark likes video games and some water sports. If he had his druthers, he would find a way to tour Europe someday.

How Mark Could Navigate His Pit of Success

- **Hotwire his changeable brain:** Mark could ask himself if his brain can learn to advise these clients. He could assess if he is using any self-talk that discounts his ability to learn or provide value. He could also start asking himself, "I wonder how I can learn what I need," and then write down the answers.

- **Embrace the pit:** In addition to reviewing why the work is important for clients and for himself, Mark could think about what he can give to clients. He could identify what he could learn, deciding on one or two skills in particular. He might also ask some of the senior consultants to share how they have started client relationships.
- **Trade up (and up):** Mark could examine whether he is overly focused on *should* or on *fear*. After naming what he is feeling, he could look for a way to replace any out-of-control feelings with what he can control. He needs to focus on what he wants to give to clients rather than what he wants from them.
- **Make something from nothing:** Mark can ask himself, "What problem am I trying to solve?" One answer might be that he wants to help clients solve their problems. As he gets clear on the problem, he will want to ask what resources he has or can obtain to help solve those problems.
- **Slow down to speed up:** When he feels overwhelmed in meetings, Mark can ask himself, "What do I need?" He may also think long-term and start planning a trip to Europe for next summer. In the shorter term, he could visit his favorite lake at the end of the month.

Case 3: Learning Beyond One's Core Expertise

Demetra is a senior marketing research analyst who has been in the business for twenty years. She received her master's degree and PhD in marketing research and is recognized by management and peers as the go-to person for analytical solutions. She has been at her current company for eight years, is well liked in and out of her department, and continually receives high performance reviews.

An organizational change has shifted the needs of the company, and researchers are being asked to expand their skill sets to move from a data collection and analysis focus to strategy and execution. Demetra and the other analysts are still expected to collect data and conduct analyses, but they are now also expected to help their internal clients think through the broader strategy implications.

Although Demetra has always done more than just hand over the data, this change requires a new type of thinking and more hands-on effort to manage relationships over a longer period. Success now includes helping the company's clients create strategies with the data and implement the findings.

During the four months that the change has been in place, Demetra has made little progress on adapting to a more strategic focus. She is not opposed to the idea, but she does not see herself as wired to think in this strategic way. After all, people like what she does.

Demetra has visited many countries around the world. She loves art museums and periodically takes a painting class. She is divorced and spends her evenings and weekends taking her ten-year-old daughter to soccer games and practice.

How Demetra Could Navigate Her Pit of Success

- **Hotwire her changeable brain:** Demetra might ask herself what she would do if she believed her brain could change to focus more on strategy. After self-assessing whether she is using any language that is unfriendly to her brain, she could find a small way to move forward.
- **Embrace the pit:** Demetra should articulate her purpose: why does she need to navigate through this pit of success?

She can focus more on discovery and can narrow her scope of activities so that she has space to learn new skills.

- **Trade up (and up):** Although it is difficult for Demetra to immediately trade up to completely believe in her ability to change, she could consider what small trades she could make. She could trade her outright skepticism and avoidance for what-if thinking.

- **Make something from nothing:** Demetra can remind herself that what she needs is within her reach. The answer to the question "What problem am I trying to solve?" could be something like "Help clients think more strategically with the data." Demetra might brainstorm options to help her clients think and act more strategically.

- **Slow down to speed up:** Demetra could consider adding art to her work environment to help her feel at peace in the midst of her pit of success. Taking short breaks during the day could also help. She could consider taking a day off to connect with her personal purpose and take a painting class with her daughter.

Case 4: "This Is the Way We Have Always Done It"

Morey has left a large biotech company that he worked at for seven years for a smaller firm where he hopes to have greater responsibility and more influence on the direction and strategy. He believes that his experience in the previous multinational company will allow him to bring a great tool set to this new firm that wants to expand its market share.

The new company has been in business for twenty years, with its headquarters in Chicago, subsidiaries in five states, and a satellite office in Berlin. The subsidiary that Morey heads is in Denver.

Morey has received complaints about the product from a few customers, and he completely agrees with their concerns. He took the issues to the team and discussed the need for a different approach to quality control. The team members, however, adamantly defend what they have been doing. They cannot even see why anything needs to change for only a few customers. In their opinion, their process has been just fine for several years.

Morey initially gently nudges the team that even if a few customers are not getting what they need, it is a real issue. He does not want to be the new guy bulldozing a new approach, but he knows from his experience that this quality-control issue could lead to bigger issues. Nor is this the only process that the team seems to believe is good enough.

He goes home every night feeling as if he has hit a brick wall with getting the team to see the big picture. In spite of his senior role at the company subsidiary, he feels stuck. Since taking the job, he has spent his evenings and weekends working on understanding the company rather than doing anything for himself.

How Morey Could Navigate His Pit of Success

- **Hotwire his changeable brain:** He needs to make sure that the words he uses to describe himself and the teams are brain friendly. He should remind himself that his team members have changeable brains, but the more common tendency is to stick to their current expertise. Because they are wired to repeat what they have always done, he needs to find small actions to get them started on a new pathway.

Morey should also remember that he is not supposed to already know how to do all this.

- **Embrace the pit:** To learn how to coach people who are resistant, Morey needs to clarify purpose for both himself and the business. The focus should be on discovery rather than on forcing change. And instead of adding other things to be addressed, Morey should narrow the scope of changes in the business.

- **Trade up (and up):** Morey should interrupt his thoughts of being stuck and find a different focus. By seeking to understand the team's existing processes, he may learn why they do it the current way. He can identify ways that the team can hear directly from customers. He needs to ask himself what things he can control and help others see what they can control. He should also spend time clarifying his own purpose as well as his teams'. Other helpful actions are seeking help from internal people who agree with the need to change and from an expert on how to make change easier for people.

- **Make something from nothing:** At this point, Morey may assume that he has no options. To address this unhelpful attitude, he should ask himself what key problem he is trying to solve and think harder about any resources and options he has available. He can also help his team members do the same thing—get clear on what problem they are trying to solve so that they can understand the need to change.

- **Slow down to speed up:** Morey could benefit from taking time for a walk or bike ride in the evening, as he did before he took this job. He could also plan some walking meetings during the workday.

CHAPTER 11

A Ten-Week Action Plan for Your Pit

S tart improving your ability to navigate the pit of success by experimenting with the concepts provided in this action plan. The plan consists of thought questions and activities for each week. Each week follows the flow of the chapters in the book, but some weeks include more than one chapter.

How to use the Action Plan

1. Read the questions at the beginning of each week.
2. Check in with the questions every couple of days to record your answers.
3. At the end of the week, add your experiences and thoughts.
4. Proceed to the next week's questions and repeat the process.

Periodically, you may want to return to a previous week's questions, or you may want to extend a week's assignments over several weeks.

Research has shown that the act of journaling improves your ability to manage demands. So, whether you are writing down answers to this action plan or are recording your own ideas in a different way, you will increase your ability to navigate the pit by recording your thoughts in some way.

Week 1: What Pits Have You Faced?

1. Thinking about the last five years, list some activities, experiences, and projects you were involved with.

_____

_____

_____

_____

_____

_____

2. List three to five obstacles you faced (technical, mechanical, social, team, strategic, interpersonal, etc.) and how you overcame those obstacles (through effort, patience, practice, study, help, trial and error, focus, luck, etc.).

_____

_____

_____

_____

_____

_____

_____

3. Consider what you learned about any of these topics (or other topics):

Priorities	*Cultures*	*Conflict management*
Strategy	*Delegating*	*Competing demands*
Motivation	*Running meetings*	*Influence*
Relationships	*Celebrating*	*Customers*
Supply chain	*Following up*	*Yourself*
Technical expertise	*Receiving feedback*	*People*
Technology	*Giving feedback*	*Momentum*
Policy	*Decisions*	*Innovation*
Politics	*Budgets*	*Getting buy-in*
Practice	*Mistakes*	*Balance*

_____

_____

_____

_____

_____

4. What are you proud to have figured out, learned, or achieved?

_____

_____

_____

_____

_____

5. What advice would you pass on if someone were facing similar challenges?

_____

_____

_____

_____

_____

Week 2: Assessing Your Current Pits of Success

1. Describe a pit you are currently facing.

_____

_____

_____

_____

_____

2. Describe a new capability, mindset, or knowledge you need to gain.

_____

_____

_____

_____

_____

3. Describe how it feels in this pit of success.

_____

_____

_____

_____

_____

4. Describe what purpose or purposes make this pit worth going through.

_____

_____

_____

_____

_____

5. What current expertise and future expertise are you between?

_____

_____

_____

_____

_____

6. List three ways you can focus on discovery while moving toward your desired new expertise.

_____

_____

_____

_____

_____

Week 3: Understanding Your Relationship with Your Brain

1. Name one or two skills you believe you can learn by changing your brain, and one or two situations in which you have a hard time believing your brain can change.

   _____

   _____

   _____

2. Reflect on the last time you faced a setback or other challenge. What language did you use to describe yourself, the situation, and the challenges you faced? What brain-friendly phrases did you use?

   _____

   _____

   _____

3. Try some brain-friendly phrases through the week, such as these:
   - I do not have this yet.
   - I wonder how I will learn.
   - I do not understand this. What do I want to learn?
   - This is going to require multiple attempts. That is normal.
   - Practice is my path.

   _____

   _____

   _____

4. Take a small step by learning something new (it could be related or unrelated to your current pit), and notice what you say to yourself about your ability to learn.

_____

_____

_____

_____

_____

5. List what you would do if you believed your brain had nearly unlimited capability to change and grow.

_____

_____

_____

_____

_____

Week 4: Finding Your Building Blocks

1. Describe a skill you need to navigate your current pit.

_____

_____

_____

_____

_____

_____

_____

2. List some of the building blocks needed for that skill. (See Appendix B, "Identify Your Building Blocks," for more help with this step: estimating, asking for advice, seeking research or training, or jumping in.)

_____

_____

_____

_____

_____

_____

_____

3. Define the subtasks of the building blocks.

_____

_____

_____

_____

_____

4. Decide which building block you want to start with.

_____

_____

_____

_____

_____

5. Choose some brain-friendly phrases you can use as you focus on these building blocks (e.g., "This skill is learnable").

_____

_____

_____

_____

_____

Week 5: Continuing to Embrace the Pit

1. Review your purpose for going through the pit. Why do you need to navigate it?

_____

_____

_____

_____

2. What have you learned so far as you embraced this pit (e.g., lessons about the pit, your purpose, the desired skills, your current expertise, building blocks, brain-friendly language, and taking small steps)?

_____

_____

_____

_____

_____

3. Label the pit you are experiencing as a "between" space. Describe the betweenness you are experiencing.

_____

_____

_____

_____

4. Decide what you can spend less time doing so that you have more time for learning the building blocks.

---

5. Make a list of people who can help you navigate this pit.

---

6. Request guidance and feedback from someone who can provide useful insights as well as encouragement.

Week 6: Reviewing and Trading Up

1. Reflect on what you learned from seeking feedback and help. Do you need additional guidance or support?

_____

_____

_____

_____

_____

2. Consider the language you use to describe yourself when things are difficult or when you make a mistake. Is there a more brain-friendly way to describe your situation?

_____

_____

_____

_____

3. Practice "naming it" when you find yourself over-whelmed.

_____

_____

_____

_____

4. Practice "interrupting it" when you find yourself focusing on the wrong thing.

_____

_____

_____

_____

_____

_____

_____

5. Consider how you may be focusing on any of these five limiters (or any other limiter). When do you tend to focus on these? How is this limiting focus affecting you?

- Focusing on *stuck*
- Focusing on *should*
- Focusing on *hurt*
- Focusing on *fear*
- Focusing on *justified*

_____

_____

_____

_____

_____

_____

6. During the week, catch yourself focusing on one of the above-mentioned limiters. Trade up from these by asking yourself any of the following questions:

- What *is* really happening?
- What is my purpose or direction?
- What can I learn or discover?
- What can I control or influence?
- What if I could do ___? What if I had ___?
- What am I grateful for?
- What small action can I take?

_____

_____

_____

_____

_____

_____

_____

Week 7: Trading Up

1. Identify three situations where you traded up your focus this week.

   _____

   _____

   _____

   _____

2. It is important to focus on what you can control rather than on what you cannot. List which things you can control. Which ones do you want to focus on this week? What are other small ways you can trade up this week?

   _____

   _____

   _____

   _____

3. Write down the building blocks are you focusing on. What new skills have you learned so far?

   _____

   _____

   _____

   _____

   _____

Week 8: Creating Options

1. Brainstorm twenty-five ways you can use a paper clip or a drinking glass. Keep working on this list throughout the week until you come up with twenty-five. Bonus round: Can you come up with fifty?

_____

_____

_____

_____

2. Take a work problem and come up with ten different ways the situation could be improved or solved.

_____

_____

_____

_____

3. As you face situations where you feel *stuck*, practice the phrase "What I need is within my reach."

_____

_____

_____

_____

4. Apply the following tools to solve a problem you are facing:

- Define the problem: "What problem am I trying to solve?"
- Ask leading questions: "What do I want to happen?"
- Magnify your resources and options:
  - Assess: "What do I already have?"
  - Repurpose: "How can I use what I have in new ways?"
  - Expand: "How can I add resources (time, materials, skills, funding, people, etc.)?"
- Experiment: "How can I quickly discover if an option will work?"

_____

_____

_____

_____

_____

_____

_____

Week 9: Slowing Down to Speed Up

1. Describe your current approach to taking care of your brain.

   _____

   _____

   _____

   _____

   _____

2. Consider what holds you back from taking short breaks. What would need to change for you to build in more breaks?

   _____

   _____

   _____

   _____

   _____

3. Identify three specific times when you are likely to experience stress. Prepare two or three ways to respond to the upcoming demands.

   _____

   _____

   _____

   _____

4. As you experience moments of stress, ask yourself these questions:

- What am I feeling?
- What do I need (connection, quiet, rest, nourishment, movement, challenges, clarity, beauty, etc.)? (See Appendix C, "Ninety-Nine Ways to Take Care of Yourself," for more ideas.)
- What do I want to do about it?

_____

_____

_____

_____

_____

_____

Week 10: Celebrating a Victory, and Continuing the Journey

1. List the obstacles you have overcome in your journey. How did you overcome them?

_____

_____

_____

_____

_____

2. List some brain-friendly language you can continue to use this week whenever you feel overwhelmed.

_____

_____

_____

_____

3. Take time this week to teach someone else about the pit of success.

_____

_____

_____

_____

4. What is your current mindset for navigating your pits of success?

_____

_____

_____

_____

_____

5. Celebrate your new abilities in a way that is right for you.

_____

_____

_____

_____

_____

APPENDICES

Appendix A

Origins of the Pit of Success

When I (Dave) was in my doctoral program, I submitted a thirty-page proposal for my dissertation research. My committee chairman returned it with the words "Not good enough." I tried to get clarity on what he wanted, but he only gave vague answers. After several more rejections of revised proposals, I realized that my efforts were going nowhere. I "fired" him as my committee chair (not the wisest move when your chair is the head of the department). The previous six months of effort were now lost, and I had to start over. I did not realize it at the time, but I had just entered a new pit of success.

I approached one of my other professors—Glenn Richardson—who was doing pioneering research on the resiliency process model. I got excited about what he was doing, and I refocused my research. I formed a new committee and wrote a proposal that was approved. I conducted research that demonstrated that resilience was not only learnable, but also sustainable, and the foundations of the pit of success were established.

As I began to evolve the pit of success for business, I was influenced by the Center for Creative Leadership's research on learning agility, Harvard Professor Linda Hill's research on leaders who need to master new identities, change expert William Bridges' research on managing transitions, and Carol Dweck's research on the malleable brain. Working with leaders in business and government, I uncovered nuances of the pit that applied to broad leadership issues. I found implications for leading organizational change, onboarding new managers, succession planning, dealing with acquisitions and mergers, promoting innovation, and implementing strategy. All these scenarios required managers to let go of some part of their current expertise and embrace the unknowns of the pit of success.

As I taught the pit of success in Asia, Europe, the Middle East, Africa, Australia, North America, and South America, a common experience emerged among leaders: they felt unburdened when they understood the pit. Leaders of different countries, positions, ages, and education all had similar experiences. Understanding the pit of success made their challenges easier. Seeing the hope in their eyes as they learned about the pit and seeing them achieve new levels of expertise have been two of the real joys of my life.

All of this came about because I was told my work was "not good enough." I had to be thrown into a pit to discover the pit of success. Although I was not grateful at the time, I am so grateful now.

Identifying Your Building Blocks

n Chapter 2, we discussed the importance of finding and developing building blocks to accelerate your learning. No matter how big the skill or challenge, you can always break it down into building blocks that are easier to learn. When you take care of these foundational building blocks, other skills come more quickly.

In this appendix, we present four different approaches for finding the building blocks you need:

- estimate
- seek advice
- get training
- jump in

We also provide an example of the estimating approach: big to little and little to big.

Estimate (guess)	• What are the major tasks or skills needed (e.g., before, during, after)? • What are the subtasks that go into each of the tasks? • Alternatively, list the knowledge, skill, ability, relationships, or supplies that are needed to accomplish the task, and sort these items.
Seek advice	• Ask around to find out who is good at the task. • Ask topic experts for the next steps and key skills. • Ask for advice on developing the needed skills. • Ask for feedback on where you should focus.
Get training	• Take a class. (Good ones define the building blocks for you.) • Do an internet search for steps on the topics. • Read books on the topic.
Jump in	• Embrace trial and error. • Intentionally look for the small skills needed. • Identify obstacles or frustration points. • Estimate the building blocks as you go.

Estimating Approach

To find building blocks by estimating, try either of these two methods.

The Big-to-Little Approach

As you think about the pit of success in front of you, try to break it down into large categories. Then, identify which subtasks are needed for each of those categories.

Here are a few categories you might use:

- Step 1, 2, 3
- Before, during, after
- First, second, third
- Physical, mental, social, technological
- Materials, skills, knowledge, support

<u>*Example*</u>
What do you want to learn? How to lead meetings
What are the major tasks (before, during, and after) of leading a meeting?

1. Organizing the meeting
2. Running the meeting
3. Following up after the meeting

What are the subtasks for each major task?

1. *Organizing the meeting:* scheduling the meeting, getting the right people in the room, sending invitations, creating an agenda, sharing the agenda, obtaining and preparing supplies (markers, flip chart, etc.), ensuring the availability of key parties, and reserving a room
2. *Running the meeting:* reviewing the agenda, summarizing decisions, making sure everyone is heard, and managing detours
3. *Following up after the meeting:* sending out minutes, confirming that people have taken action, and following up on loose ends

The Little-to-Big-Approach

If you are having a hard time thinking about big-picture categories, try brainstorming some of the tasks involved. You can write a list or sketch it out. Once you have these smaller tasks written out, it can be then helpful to group them (as much as possible) into larger categories.

Sort the items into similar areas, and determine the category titles.

1. Scheduling the meeting, getting the right people in the room, sending invitations, creating an agenda, sharing the agenda, ensuring the availability of key parties, reserving a room, and obtaining and preparing supplies (markers, flip chart, etc.) → Organizing the meeting

2. Reviewing the agenda, summarizing decisions, making sure everyone gets heard, and managing detours → Running the meeting

3. Sending out minutes, confirming that people have taken action, and following up on loose ends → Following up after the meeting

You can also break this process down another level and divide the subtasks into smaller pieces. For example, if you found that you need to manage people who are detouring the meeting, you might break down that skill into several smaller tasks: understanding the person's point of view, setting ground rules, interrupting appropriately, and putting ideas in a "parking lot" for future discussion. Each of those tasks is a skill you can develop.

When you create your building blocks, writing them down reduces your mental burden. You know which blocks you are already good at, which ones you need to focus on, and which you are intentionally ignoring for now.

If you are unsure about how to estimate the building blocks, you may want to use other approaches (seeking advice, getting training, or jumping in) to determine what building blocks you need to focus on. Once you think you have the big picture, it is time to select which block you will focus on first. Remember, you will learn faster as you narrow your focus.

Appendix C

Ninety-Nine Ways to Take Care of Yourself

Most people have a few go-to options to take care of their brain and themselves in the midst of a pit of success. Expanding your options increases your energy, confidence, health, hope, and results. When you ask yourself, "What can I do to take care of my needs?" consider some of these ideas, and add your own.

Connection

- Do a favorite thing.
- Seek a nostalgic experience.
- Savor a moment.
- Talk with a friend.
- Socialize.
- Ask for help.
- Be fully present.
- Learn about other people.
- Call someone who makes you laugh.
- Write a thank you letter.
- Share a need with someone who can help.
- Write in a journal.
- Listen more purposefully.
- Volunteer.
- Stop multitasking.
- Share a mealtime with a friend.
- Fully empathize with another's situation.

Quiet/Rest

- Breathe (always a good choice).
- Wander.
- Close your eyes.
- Stop moving.
- Reserve one day a week to stay away from technology, phone, email, news, people, duties, TV, cooking, etc.
- Do something unrelated to your current task.
- Sleep.
- Nap.
- Meditate.
- Take some alone time.
- Daydream.
- Sit.
- Have a no-activity weekend.

Nourishment

- Get a massage.
- Drink more water.
- Have healthy snacks available.
- Read a book for fun.
- Eat fruits.
- Go out to eat.
- Get appropriate protein and carbohydrates.
- Eat vegetables.
- Enjoy a favorite treat.
- Have some chocolate.
- Go to a spa.
- Cook for yourself.

Movement

- Dance.
- Explore.
- Walk/meander.
- Stand.
- Swim.
- Play a sport.
- Do a one-minute workout.
- Walk on treadmill for five minutes.
- Run.
- Hike.
- Bike.
- Canoe.
- Paddle board.
- Stretch.
- Lift weights.
- Take the stairs.
- Do yoga.
- Go rock climbing.

Challenge

- Try a new activity.
- Start something.
- Finish something.
- Give yourself a physical challenge.
- Try a social connection that pushes you.
- Cook something new.
- Do something familiar but in a new way.
- Do something hard for you.
- Seek feedback.
- Try a mental challenge.
- Master a new topic.
- Face a fear.

Clarity

- Find a purpose.
- Establish boundaries.
- Decide criteria for your personal space needs.
- Define experiences you want to have.
- Decide things you do not what to pursue.
- Learn when to say no.
- Set goals.
- Create a short-term goal.
- Establish your priorities.
- Celebrate your accomplishments.
- Create a vision board.
- Remove one thing off your to-do list.

Beauty

- Gaze at a fountain.
- Study a leaf.
- Notice the architecture around you.
- Listen to music.
- Take a walk in a park.
- Enjoy the sun set.
- Watch the moon rise.
- Walk next to a stream.
- Stroll on a beach, or imagine the stroll.
- Visit an art gallery.
- Clean up your surroundings.
- Organize an area.
- Visit the mountains.
- Look for falling stars.
- Go on a favorite drive.

Notes

Chapter 1

1. Shirley, D. S., and Askwith, R. (2017). *Let It Go: The Memoirs of Dame Stephanie Shirley*. Andrews UK Limited.
2. Zetlin, M. (2019, September 20). "Blockbuster Could Have Bought Netflix for $50 Million, but the CEO Thought It Was a Joke." *Inc.* Retrieved September 17, 2020, from www.inc.com/minda-zetlin/netflix-blockbuster-meeting-marc-randolph-reed-hastings-john-antioco.html.
3. Christensen, C. M. (2013). *The Innovator's Dilemma: When New Technologies Cause Great Firms to Fail*. Harvard Business Review Press.
4. Clark, Timothy R. (2010). *EPIC change: How to Lead Change in the Global Age*. John Wiley & Sons.

Chapter 2

1. Martins, A., and Rincon, P. (2014, June 12). "Paraplegic in Robotic Suit Kicks Off World Cup." *BBC News.* Retrieved

August 17, 2020, from www.bbc.com/news/science-environment-27812218.

2. Bhattacharya, Ananya. "Paraplegics Are Learning to Walk Again with Virtual Reality." *Quartz*, Quartz, 18 Aug. 2016, qz.com/757516/paraplegics-are-learning-to-walk-again-with-virtual-reality/.

3. Ericsson, K. A., Krampe, R. T., and Tesch-Römer, C. (1993). "The Role of Deliberate Practice in the Acquisition of Expert Performance." *Psychological Review*, 100(3), 363.

4. Rock, D. (2010). "Your Brain at Work: Strategies for Overcoming Distraction, Regaining Focus, and Working Smarter All Day Long." *Journal of Behavioral Optometry*, 21(5), 130.

5. Begley, S. (2012). *The Plastic Mind.* Hachette UK.

6. Maguire, E. A., Gadian, D. G., Johnsrude, I. S., Good, C. D., Ashburner, J., Frackowiak, R. S., and Frith, C. D. (2000). "Navigation-Related Structural Change in the Hippocampi of Taxi Drivers." *Proceedings of the National Academy of Sciences*, 97(8), 4398–4403.

7. Voelcker-Rehage, C., and Willimczik, K. (2006). "Motor Plasticity in a Juggling Task in Older Adults—A Developmental Study." *Age and Ageing*, 35(4), 422–427.

8. Merabet, L. B., and Pascual-Leone, A. (2010). "Neural Reorganization Following Sensory Loss: The Opportunity of Change." *Nature Reviews Neuroscience*, 11(1), 44–52.

9. Mahncke, H. W., Bronstone, A., and Merzenich, M. M. (2006). "Brain Plasticity and Functional Losses in the Aged: Scientific Bases for a Novel Intervention." *Progress in Brain Research*, 157, 81–109.

10. Mahncke, H. W., Connor, B. B., Appelman, J., Ahsanuddin, O. N., Hardy, J. L., Wood, R. A., Joyce, N. M., Boniske,

T., Atkins, S. M., and Merzenich, M. M. (2006). "Memory Enhancement in Healthy Older Adults Using a Brain Plasticity-Based Training Program: A Randomized, Controlled Study." *Proceedings of the National Academy of Sciences,* 103(33), 12523–12528.

11. Deckersbach, T., Das, S. K., Urban, L. E., Salinardi, T., Batra, P., Rodman, A. M., Arulpragasam, A. R., Dougherty, D. D., and Roberts, S. B. (2014). "Pilot Randomized Trial Demonstrating Reversal of Obesity-Related Abnormalities in Reward System Responsivity to Food Cues with a Behavioral Intervention." *Nutrition & Diabetes,* 4(9), e129–e129.

12. Dweck, C. S. (2000). *Self-Theories: Their Role in Motivation, Personality, and Development.* Psychology Press.

13. Dweck, C. S. (2008). *Mindset: The New Psychology of Success.* Random House Digital.

14. Bloom, B. S. (1981). *All Our Children Learning: A Primer for Parents, Teachers, and Other Educators.* McGraw-Hill Companies.

15. Bloom, B. S. (1984). "The 2 Sigma Problem: The Search for Methods of Group Instruction as Effective as One-to-One Tutoring." *Educational Researcher,* 13(6), 4–16.

16. Levine, D. U. (1985). *Improving Student Achievement Through Mastery Learning Programs.* Jossey-Bass.

17. Anderson, Lorin W. (1975, March). "Major Assumptions of Mastery Learning." Presentation at Annual Meeting of the Southeast Psychological Association, Atlanta.

18. *Los Angeles Times.* "At 98, No-Longer-Illiterate Man Turns the Page." (2000, February 6). Retrieved October 12, 2020 from www.latimes.com/archives/la-xpm-2000-feb-06-mn-61546-story.html.

19. Newberg, A., and Waldman, M. R. (2013). *Words Can Change Your Brain: 12 Conversation Strategies to Build Trust, Resolve Conflict, and Increase Intimacy.* Penguin.
20. Fogg, B. J. (2019). *Tiny Habits: The Small Changes That Change Everything.* Houghton Mifflin Harcourt.
21. Sapolsky, R. M. (2017). *Behave: The Biology of Humans at Our Best and Worst.* Penguin.

Chapter 3

1. Siler, K. (2010). "Social and Psychological Challenges of Poker." *Journal of Gambling Studies*, 26(3), 401–420.
2. Duckworth, Angela (2016). *Grit: The Power of Passion and Perseverance.* Vol. 234. New York, NY: Scribner.
3. Deloitte. (2014). "Culture of Purpose—Building Business Confidence; Driving Growth: 2014 Core Beliefs & Culture Survey." Retrieved October 2, 2020, from www2.deloitte.com/content/dam/Deloitte/global/Documents/About-Deloitte/gx-culture-of-purpose.pdf.
4. Kessler, D. (2020). *Finding Meaning: The Sixth Stage of Grief.* Scribner.
5. Latham, G. P., and Seijts, G. H. (1999). "The Effects of Proximal and Distal Goals on Performance on a Moderately Complex Task." *Journal of Organizational Behavior*, 20(4), 421–429.
6. Yeager, D. S., Walton, G. M., Brady, S. T., Akcinar, E. N., Paunesku, D., Keane, L., Kamentz,D., Ritter, G., Duckworth, A. L., Urstein, R., Gomez, E. M., Markus, H. R., Cohen, G. L., and Dweck, C. S. (2016). "Teaching a Lay Theory Before College Narrows Achievement Gaps at Scale." *Proceedings of the National Academy of Sciences*, 113(24), E3341–E3348.

7. VandeWalle, D., Brown, S. P., Cron, W. L., and Slocum, J. W. Jr. (1999). "The Influence of Goal Orientation and Self-Regulation Tactics on Sales Performance: A Longitudinal Field Test." *Journal of Applied Psychology*, 84(2), 249.

8. Dweck, C. S., and Leggett, E. L. (1988). "A Social-Cognitive Approach to Motivation and Personality." *Psychological Review*, 95(2), 256.

9. Latham, G. P., and Ernst, C. T. (2006). "Keys to Motivating Tomorrow's Workforce." *Human Resource Management Review*, 16(2), 181–198.

10. Seijts, G., Taylor, L., and Latham, G. (1998). "Enhancing Teaching Performance Through Goal Setting, Implementation and Seeking Feedback." *International Journal for Academic Development*, 3(2), 156–168.

11. Olvera-Cortés, M. E., Anguiano-Rodríguez, P., López-Vázquez, M. Á., and Alfaro, J. M. C. (2008). "Serotonin/Dopamine Interaction in Learning." *Progress in Brain Research*, 172, 567–602.

12. Howe, M. W., Tierney, P. L., Sandberg, S. G., Phillips, P. E., and Graybiel, A. M. (2013). "Prolonged Dopamine Signaling in Striatum Signals Proximity and Value of Distant Rewards." *Nature*, 500(7464), 575–579.

13. McChesney, C., Covey, S., and Huling, J. (2012). *The 4 Disciplines of Execution: Achieving Your Wildly Important Goals.* Simon & Schuster.

14. Lehmann, A. C., and Ericsson, K. A. (1997). "Research on Expert Performance and Deliberate Practice: Implications for the Education of Amateur Musicians and Music Students." *Psychomusicology: A Journal of Research in Music Cognition*, 16(1–2), 40.

15. Brooks, A. W., Gino, F., and Schweitzer, M. E. (2015). "Smart People Ask for (My) Advice: Seeking Advice Boosts Perceptions of Competence." *Management Science*, 61(6), 1421–1435.

16. Abel, J. R., and Deitz, R. (2015). "Agglomeration and Job Matching Among College Graduates." *Regional Science and Urban Economics*, 51, 14–24.

Chapter 4

1. Rudetsky, S. (2017, May 15). "What Happened When Audra McDonald Flubbed Her Lyrics in Front of Stephen Sondheim?" *Playbill*. Retrieved August 17, 2020, from www.playbill.com/article/what-happened-when-audra-mcdonald-flubbed-her-lyrics-in-front-of-stephen-sondheim.

2. Black, J. S., and Gregersen, H. B. (2002). *Leading Strategic Change: Breaking Through the Brain Barrier*. FT Press.

3. Lewis, R. B. (2007, July). "The Art of Strafing." *Air Force Magazine*. Retrieved September 14, 2020, from www.airforcemag.com/PDF/MagazineArchive/Documents/2007/July%202007/0707strafing.pdf.

Chapter 5

1. *Huffington Post*, from KTLA TV. (2017, December 7). "Local Teen Uses Craigslist to Trade Cell Phone for Porsche." Retrieved September 10, 2020, from www.huffpost.com/entry/steven-ortiz-local-teen-t_n_654246.

2. Wiseman, R. (2004). *The Luck Factor*. Random House.

3. Dyer, J. H., Gregersen, H. B., and Christensen, C. M. (2009, December). "The Innovator's DNA." *Harvard Business Review*, 87.

4. Astle, D. E., and Scerif, G. (2009). "Using Developmental Cognitive Neuroscience to Study Behavioral and Attentional Control." *Developmental Psychobiology*, 51(2), 107–118.

5. Lisitsa, E. (2013, April 26). "The Four Horsemen: The Antidotes." Retrieved September 17, 2020, from www.gottman.com/blog/the-four-horsemen-the-antidotes.

6. Lieberman, M. D., Eisenberger, N. I., Crockett, M. J., Tom, S. M., Pfeifer, J. H., and Way, B. M. (2007). "Affect Labeling Disrupts Amygdala Activity in Response to Affective Stimuli." *Psychological Science*, 18(5), 421–428.

7. Siegel, D. J., and Bryson, T. P. (2012). *The Whole-Brain Child: 12 Revolutionary Strategies to Nurture Your Child's Developing Mind*. Bantam.

Chapter 6

1. Woods, W. D., Kemppanen, J., Turhanov, A., and Waugh, L. J., eds. "Day 3, Part 2: 'Houston, We've Had a Problem.'" Apollo 13 Flight Journal, National Aeronautics and Space Administration. Retrieved August 2, 2020, from https://history.nasa.gov/afj/ap13fj/08day3-problem.html.

2. Diaz, J. (2018, September 4). "This Is the Actual Hack That Saved the Astronauts of the Apollo XIII." *Gizmodo*. Retrieved September 10, 2020, from https://gizmodo.com/this-is-the-actual-hack-that-saved-the-astronauts-of-th-1598385593.

3. Lovell, J. (n.d.). "'Houston, We've Had a Problem,'" in *Apollo Expeditions to the Moon*, chapter 13. National Aeronautics and Space Administration. Retrieved September 10, 2020, from https://history.nasa.gov/SP-350/ch-13-1.html.

4. Rock, D. (2009, November 8). "A Sense of Autonomy Is a Primary Reward or Threat for the Brain." *Psychology Today*.

Retrieved September 11, 2020, from www.psychologytoday.
com/us/blog/your-brain-work/200911/sense-autonomy-is-pri-
mary-reward-or-threat-the-brain.

5. Marmot, M. G., Bosma, H., Hemingway, H., Brunner, E., and
   Stansfeld, S. (1997). "Contribution of Job Control and Other
   Risk Factors to Social Variations in Coronary Heart Disease
   Incidence." *Lancet*, 350(9073), 235–239.

6. Maier, Steven F., and Linda R. Watkins. "Stressor Control-
   lability and Learned Helplessness: The Roles of the Dorsal
   Raphe Nucleus, Serotonin, and Corticotropin-releasing
   Factor." *Neuroscience & Biobehavioral Reviews* 29.4-5
   (2005): 829-841.

7. Maier, S. F., & Seligman, M. E. (2016). Learned Helplessness at Fifty: Insights from Neuroscience. *Psychological
   Review*, *123*(4), 349.

8. Douglas Bremner, J. (2006). "Stress and Brain Atrophy." *CNS
   & Neurological Disorders—Drug Targets [Formerly Current
   Drug Targets—CNS & Neurological Disorders]*, 5(5), 503–512.

9. Hiroto, D. S., and Seligman, M. E. (1975). "Generality of
   Learned Helplessness in Man." *Journal of Personality and
   Social Psychology* 31(2), 311.

10. Dyer, J. (2020, June). Interview with author (Dave Jennings).

11. Associated Press. (2006, December 14). "World's Tallest Man
    Saves Dolphins in China." *NBC News*. Retrieved September
    17, 2020, from www.nbcnews.com/id/16203273/ns/world_
    news-wonderful_world/t/worlds-tallest-man-saves-dolphins-
    china.

12. Medina, J. (2011). *Brain Rules: 12 Principles for Surviving
    and Thriving at Work, Home, and School.* Pear Press.

13. Wikipedia (2020). s.v. "MacGyver." Last updated August 21, 2020. Retrieved September 17, 2020, from https://en.wikipedia.org/wiki/MacGyver.

14. Robinson, A. (2018, March 12). "Want to Boost Your Bottom Line? Encourage Your Employees to Work on Side Projects." *Inc.* Retrieved September 17, 2020, from www.inc.com/adam-robinson/google-employees-dedicate-20-percent-of-their-time-to-side-projects-heres-how-it-works.html.

Chapter 7

1. El-bashir, T. (1999, February 16). "For a Lack of Pit Stop, a Big Race Was Lost." *New York Times*. Retrieved September 14, 2020, from www.nytimes.com/1999/02/16/sports/auto-racing-for-a-lack-of-pit-stop-a-big-race-was-lost.html.

2. Jabr, F. (2013, October 15). "Why Your Brain Needs More Downtime." *Scientific American*. Retrieved September 14, 2020, from www.scientificamerican.com/article/mental-downtime.

3. Bronson, P., and Merryman, A. (2009). *NurtureShock: New Thinking About Children*. Twelve.

4. Peters, Achim. "The Selfish Brain: Competition for Energy Resources." *American Journal of Human Biology* 23.1 (2011): 29-34.

5. Stachenfeld, N. S., Leone, C. A., Mitchell, E. S., Freese, E., and Harkness, L. (2018). "Water Intake Reverses Dehydration Associated Impaired Executive Function in Healthy Young Women." *Physiology & Behavior*, 185, 103–111.

6. Wittbrodt, M. T., and Millard-Stafford, M. (2018). "Dehydration Impairs Cognitive Performance: A Meta-analysis." *Medicine & Science in Sports & Exercise*, 50(11), 2360–2368.

7. Huffington, A. (2017, April 06). "10 Years Ago I Collapsed From Burnout and Exhaustion, and It's the Best Thing That Could Have Happened to Me." *Medium.* Retrieved September 11, 2020, from https://medium.com/thrive-global/10-years-ago-i-collapsed-from-burnout-and-exhaustion-and-its-the-best-thing-that-could-have-b1409f16585d.

8. Raeburn, P. (2014, May 9). "Arianna Huffington: Collapse from Exhaustion Was 'Wake-Up Call.'" *Today.* Retrieved September 11, 2020, from www.today.com/health/arianna-huffington-collapse-exhaustion-was-wake-call-2D79644042.

9. Tangney, J. P., and Dearing, R. L. (2003). *Shame and Guilt.* Guilford Press.

10. Steele, M. (2020, April). Interview with author (Dave Jennings).

11. Perlow, L. A., and Porter, J. L. (2014, August 1). "Making Time Off Predictable—And Required." *Harvard Business Review.* Retrieved September 11, 2020, from https://hbr.org/2009/10/making-time-off-predictable-and-required.

12. Lee, K. E., Williams, K. J., Sargent, L. D., Williams, N. S., and Johnson, K. A. (2015). "40-Second Green Roof Views Sustain Attention: The Role of Micro-Breaks in Attention Restoration." *Journal of Environmental Psychology,* 42, 182–189.

13. Oppezzo, M., and Schwartz, D. L. (2014). "Give Your Ideas Some Legs: The Positive Effect of Walking on Creative Thinking." *Journal of Experimental Psychology: Learning, Memory, and Cognition,* 40(4): 1142.

14. Leslie, I. (2016, October 20). "The Scientists Who Make Apps Addictive." *Economist.* Retrieved September 11, 2020, from

www.economist.com/1843/2016/10/20/the-scientists-who-make-apps-addictive.

15. Fogg, B. J. (2019). *Tiny Habits: The Small Changes That Change Everything.* Houghton Mifflin Harcourt.

16. Coleman Wood, K. A., Lowndes, B. R., Buus, R. J., and Hallbeck, M. S. (2018). "Evidence-Based Intraoperative Microbreak Activities for Reducing Musculoskeletal Injuries in the Operating Room." *Work*, 60(4), 649–659.

17. Lang, S. S. (1999). "When Workers Heed Computer's Reminder to Take a Break Their Productivity Jumps, Cornell Study Finds." Cornell News.

18. Rosekind, M. R., Graeber, R. C., Dinges, D. F., Connell, L. J., Rountree, M. S., Spinweber, C. L., and Gillen, K. A. (1994, September). "Crew Factors in Flight Operations IX: Effects of Planned Cockpit Rest on Crew Performance and Alertness in Long-Haul Operations." NASA Technical Reports Server. Retrieved October 2, 2020, from https://ntrs.nasa.gov/citations/19950006379.

19. Nawijn, J., Marchand, M. A., Veenhoven, R., and Vingerhoets, A. J. (2010). "Vacationers Happier, but Most Not Happier After a Holiday." *Applied Research in Quality of Life*, 5(1), 35–47.

Chapter 8

1. Katz, J. (2009, April 09). "The Measure of Genius: Michelangelo's Sistine Chapel at 500." *Smithsonian Magazine.* Retrieved September 14, 2020, from www.smithsonianmag.com/arts-culture/the-measure-of-genius-michelangelos-sistine-chapel-at-500-123313873.

2. The quote—*If people knew how hard I had to work to gain my mastery, it would not seem so wonderful at all*—is often attributed to Michelangelo. The oldest known reference suggesting he said it occurs in *Instructor, Volume 39, 1929.*

About the Authors

Dave Jennings is a leadership and organizational change consultant. He has guided leaders from across the globe to navigate the *pit of success* for themselves, their teams, and their company. He has worked with such organizations as Salesforce, Microsoft, Intel, Oracle, Deloitte, Exxon/Mobil, Schneider Electric, Myriad Genetics, Kaiser-Permanente, Alaska Airlines, and the FBI. He has been a featured speaker at leadership conferences in twenty-two countries. He is author of *Catapulted: How Great Leaders Succeed Beyond Their Experience,* and his articles and commentary have been relied on by the *Washington Post, Forbes,* and TheStreet. com. He is an adjunct instructor for Kenan-Flagler Business School's Executive Development program at the University of North Carolina. He earned his PhD researching change resilience. Contact Dave at dave@davejennings.com or learn more online at www.learnablesolutions.com and www.davejennings.com.

Amy Leishman is an executive coach, retreat facilitator, and researcher. With a focus on resilience and leadership, she empowers individuals to influence, problem solve, and set direction for the challenges they face. Additionally, her research

202 | THE PIT OF SUCCESS

interests include women in leadership, the triple bottom line, and sustainable social impact. She has helped leaders succeed in non-profit, small business, and Fortune 500 organizations. She has led market research around the globe, including work in Italy, India, Mauritius, Ecuador, Mexico, Peru, Nigeria, Thailand, and New Zealand. Her MBA was focused on Strategy and Social Innovation from Marriott School of Business. Learn more about Amy at www.learnablesolutions.com and www.amyleishman.com.

Expand the Learning

We provide in-person and virtual experiences to help leaders, teams, and businesses navigate the pit of success.

Executive Coaching: Whether leaders need to define the strategy, lead a change, or build credibility, we help them gain the mindset and skill set they need to navigate their pit and achieve success.

Strategy and Leading Change Retreats: To effectively lead their organizations through the pit of success, leadership teams must be aligned on "what is winning" and "what it takes to win." We facilitate retreats that create focus, build commitment, and deliver results.

Seminars/Training: Whether in-person or virtual, our facilitators create highly engaging experiences with pragmatic tools and concepts. We provide executive, manager, and individual contributor options.

Keynotes: The authors provide keynotes for small teams, conferences, and large organizations to help everyone embrace the pit of success and achieve greater results.

Learn more:
www.learnablesolutions.com